JO

The Way Forward

FACING SPIRITUAL WARFARE, LIVING WITH A MISSION, CONNECTING IN REAL COMMUNITY

TENTH
POWER

Elgin, IL · Tyler, TX

TENTHPOWERPUBLISHING

www.tenthpowerpublishing.com

Copyright © 2019 by Josh Brown

All rights reserved. No part of this book may be reproduced without permission from the author, except by a reviewer quoting brief passages in a review; nor may any part of this book be reproduced, stored in a retrieval system or copied by mechanical photocopying, recording or other means without written permission from the author.

Scripture quotations are from The ESV® Bible (The Holy Bible, English Standard Version®), copyright © 2001 by Crossway, a publishing ministry of Good News Publishers. Used by permission. All rights reserved.

Design by Inkwell Creative.

Softcover 978-1-938840-23-4
e-book 978-1-938840-26-5
10 9 8 7 6 5 4 3 2 1

All ministry of our Lord Jesus is done in coordination with the church, the faith community, through the work of the Holy Spirit. Therefore, first and foremost, I must thank the Triune God for his faithfulness in my redemption and throughout this process. For the gifts of my wife, Brittany, and our children, Josie and Caleb... you are my life. You are always pushing me past what I thought was possible. To Mom and Dad for your uncompromising support and love. To my brothers, Dave, Grayson, and Scott—your partnership in ministry makes me a better pastor, husband, and father. To my church family at St. Lukes—without your help, this wouldn't have been possible! To all of my brothers and sisters in Christ looking forward in this journey, thank you for your example and companionship. It is my humble privilege to walk with you.

TABLE OF CONTENTS

PREFACE

I sat in a Starbucks on the outskirts of Reno, listening as new church members Brian and Jess shared their story and cautiously opened wounds they had from previous church experiences spanning decades and multiple churches. Some scars are fresh and some are old. It's becoming a familiar story—people who have been burned by the church.

As you read the headlines echoing the voice of evangelism in America, the story is the same. People become disenfranchised by the church because of the wounds the church has inflicted.

After graduating from Concordia Seminary in 2011, I became a pastor. One of my greatest joys in ministry is these one-on-one meetings because they provide a unique opportunity to step outside of the regular schedule and do what I love: get to know people better, meet them where they are in their spiritual journey, and encourage them on their next steps. Most of my meetings are just down the street from the church at a local coffee shop. It's where I go to disengage from church-life and stay connected in the real world where everyone else lives.

My hope for this book is twofold: to apply some spiritual aloe vera to begin the healing of Christians who have been burned and disenfranchised by the church or religion, and to help the marginally connected grow deeper in their faith and faith community. I will speak about the challenges Christians face throughout their spiritual journey and offer tools for Christian living, helping them find what they need in a faith community.

INTRODUCTION

There are two parts to the task. The first is to deal with the things getting in your way on your faith journey. If sin, death, and the devil are having their way with you, it will be very hard to grow in part two. To prepare you for that growth, you will learn about the challenges you face, the lies our enemies tell, and how to find God's victory in your spiritual warfare. Part two will provide key insight into your faith journey, as it describes the nature of your relationship with God, along with the gifts he gives you in his Law and Gospel to make the journey. As you practice using God's Law and Gospel in your own life, you will learn how to use them to help others as God calls you to the mission. The last and most important thing is to help you find the right faith community to plug into. I will share some helpful hints to get you there faster. Before you get started, read Psalm 23 and reflect on David's faith journey.

Don't set out without your destination in mind. Consider what you are hoping to get out of this book. Pray, asking God to walk with you through this season of your life because it's time to enjoy faith's journey. Be ready for freedom and spiritual growth.

PSALM 23

Psalm 23 holds the title for most popular Psalm of the entire Bible. The psalm reflects David's worshipful mindset throughout his life journey. It sets the tone for his experiences—the good and the bad—and it offers a helpful lens for us to see his inward perspective, as it resonates with our own journey. This book will act as a guide to assist you in your spiritual journey, to offer insight into the green pastures and the valleys, and to remind you of the promises of God: "I will fear no evil, for *you* are with me." Read these words of David and contemplate their meaning. Look for insight into your experiences. Value them in your own journey, and hold these promises as you trust in God's faithfulness.

"The LORD is my shepherd; I shall not want. He makes me lie down in green pastures. He leads me beside still waters. He restores my soul. He leads me in paths of righteousness for his name's sake. Even though I walk through the valley of the shadow of death, I will fear no evil, for you are with me; your rod and your staff, they comfort me. You prepare a table before me in the presence of my enemies; you anoint my head with oil; my cup overflows. Surely goodness and mercy shall follow me all the days of my life, and I shall dwell in the house of the LORD forever."

—Psalm 23

Part One

What's Holding You Back?

SPIRITUAL WARFARE

T HE PROPHET ELISHA HAD A gift; he was able to see the bigger picture amidst the regular experiences of his life.

> *"Then Elisha prayed and said, 'O LORD, please open his eyes that he may see.' So the LORD opened the eyes of the young man, and he saw, and behold, the mountain was full of horses and chariots of fire all around Elisha."*

—2 Kings 6:17

Elisha had a gift. Although many might consider seeing chariots of fire an unsettling ability, I see the merits of such a gift because it's challenging to keep spiritual things (active forces at work in every moment, intertwined with the mundane day-to-day of life) at the forefront of my mind.

When I told my great-grandmother I was planning to become a pastor, she teared up. I had had visions of her swelling with pride at the thought of her grandchild going into the ministry, so this was unexpected. I asked her what was wrong and she said, "The devil is going to work so much harder on you now." A wise and faithful woman! Before she said that, I had given little thought to the devil and his work. Experience has taught me that many of us don't consider the actual danger of the situation:

> *"I'm reminded of a sobering fact: Every day, every hour, this very minute, perhaps, dark forces attempt to penetrate this castle's walls. But in the end, their greatest weapon is [...]."*

> —Albus Dumbledore, *Harry Potter and the Half Blood Prince*

Who are these dark forces? What are their greatest weapons? These are the questions that must be answered to realize the stakes. The old saying "the devil made me do it" sounds like a cop out, so understanding the tools you have and the faith community you belong to are of the utmost importance.

> *"Finally, be strong in the Lord and in the strength of his might. Put on the whole armor of God, that you may be able to stand against the schemes of the devil. For we do not wrestle against flesh and blood, but against the rulers, against the authorities, against the cosmic powers over this present darkness, against the spiritual forces of evil in the heavenly places."*

> —Ephesians 6:10–12

CHAPTER 1

Sin

Sin is not an unfamiliar word within Christian faith communities or even the greater secular culture. However, because it is such a widely used word that holds a vast portion of Christian teaching, it is hard to step past a very basic understanding of it. The children's answer, "Sin is bad," is still the most common response I get when I ask adults, "What is sin?" If we dig a little deeper, we find that most people make the connection that sin is the "bad" we do. Most Christians only connect sin with actions that are inherently bad. This is a primary issue because it is always an advantage for the enemy to be misunderstood. Without a working understanding of the nature, motivation, and tactics of our enemy, we are giving it a significant advantage over us. So it's time to take a deeper biblical look at sin and do some recon on this devastating aggressor.

The biblical language is clear as it affirms our childhood definition of sin: from Adam's adjunct leadership to Cain's jealousy and murder,

Moses' disobedience, and Aaron's pandering, let alone Ahab's idolatry and treachery. Oh, and let's not forget Manasseh's Asherah poles. There is no question that sin is seen in actions, but Jesus takes it deeper in the Sermon on the Mount, pointing out that sin isn't even isolated to actions but inhabits our thoughts, emotions, and inclinations. Jesus illustrates in stark contrast the pervasiveness of sin throughout every aspect of our lives. Paul takes it even further when he describes sin operating not as a verb but as a noun. In Romans chapter 7, Paul depicts the battle against his will and the will of sin.

> *"It was sin, producing death in me through what is good, in order that sin might be shown to be sin, and through the commandment might become sinful beyond measure. For we know that the law is spiritual, but I am of the flesh, sold under sin. For I do not understand my own actions. For I do not do what I want, but I do the very thing I hate. Now if I do what I do not want, I agree with the law, that it is good. So now it is no longer I who do it, but sin that dwells within me."*

—Romans 7:13b–17

In the second part of verse 13, you grammar buffs can brag about what most of us overlook: sin is not functioning as a verb but as the subject. Sin isn't what is being done (action); it is the one doing something (actor). Sin, in this case, is producing death. In verse 14, Paul is sold as a slave under the power of sin, a power that he cannot overcome himself, even though his will opposes sin. By verse 17, we see the nature of sin as it acts against Paul in its own interest, overpowering him and, even worse, working not as an enemy outside the gate but inside the walls. This enemy fights against us from within. From this reality Paul laments the battle, the constant struggle between his will and the evil inside that is always lurking to take advantage of any and every situation. To this entire conflict he waves the white flag and relinquishes any control he has in the outcome.

> *"For I know that nothing good dwells in me, that is, in my flesh. For I have the desire to do what is right, but not the ability to carry it out. For I do not do the good I want, but the evil I do not want is what I keep on doing. Now if I do what I do not want, it is no longer I who do it, but sin that dwells within me. So I find it to be a law that when I want to do right, evil lies close at hand. For I delight in the law of God, in my inner being, but I see in my members another law waging war against the law of my mind and making me captive to the law of sin that dwells in my members. Wretched man that I am! Who will deliver me from this body of death?"*

—Romans 7:18–25

THE JAILOR

In Rotten Tomatoes' number one movie of all time, *Shawshank Redemption*, we watch the development of the deep friendship between Andy Dufresne and Red as they support each other through the challenges and hazards of life at Shawshank Prison. In the prison there is one antagonist who is particularly scary: Captain Hadley, the blond-haired, strong-jawed captain of the guard who keeps control over the inmates through fear and force. He is cocky about his power and abusive with his authority. I realize that he is not the main antagonist and that it's Bob Gunton's character who is at the root of the abuses and is the most disturbing. However, it's Captain Hadley that gets the screen time, a character type which has been in almost every single prison movie. *Shawshank* has Hadley; *The Green Mile* has Percy; *The Longest Yard* has Knauer. It's a common theme: there is always someone who takes advantage of the system.

I call sin the Jailor to bring to your mind those characters. Sin is not just actions but is an entity working over and against you in opposition to God's love and justice. He places shackles on your wrists and ankles, puts you in a small dank cell, shuts the gate, and locks you in dark isolation where human and divine contact seem a distant memory. When you are the prisoner, it seems like the Jailor has supreme authority over your life. You are completely trapped under his domain. To be clear, sin is neither the judge nor the warden. It is only by a judge's authority that we are placed in prison. Sin doesn't have authority to incarcerate us. It is the warden's responsibility to govern and operate the prison. Sin doesn't have that right or responsibility. Sin is simply a rogue jailor seizing the opportunity given by the system to take advantage of inmates. To belabor this metaphor, I would suggest God is the judge and the warden is the Law of God (but more on this later).

Paul breaks down this relationship between God's Law and Sin in Romans 7

> *"What then shall we say? That the law is sin? By no means! Yet if it had not been for the law, I would not have known sin. For I would not have known what it is to covet if the law had not said, 'You shall not covet.' But sin, seizing an opportunity through the commandment, produced in me all kinds of covetousness. For apart from the law, sin lies dead. I was once alive apart from the law, but when the commandment came, sin came alive and I died. The very commandment that promised life proved to be death to me. For sin, seizing an opportunity through the commandment, deceived me and through it killed me. So the law is holy, and the commandment is holy and righteous and good."*

—Romans 7:7–12

There is a pervasive opinion among inmates (those of us struggling with sin) that it is the fault of the warden (the Law of God) or the judge (God himself) that they are now imprisoned. This notion is exactly what Paul is trying to help correct. Skewed beliefs like these become easy tools for another enemy to use to his advantage. Paul draws the distinction that the Law was given to maintain a healthy system for life, but through that structure, sin seized the opportunity to manipulate and dominate. We see that sin takes advantage of the good, perfect, and pleasing will of God and twists it to create an authority for itself, albeit small and perverse. Back to the metaphor, there is no prison without a warden, nor a jailor. Yet from this small position, it is able to dominate our lives to its own advantage.

SIN'S MOTIVATION

The question has to be *why*? Why does sin do all of this, working from within, continually, without reprieve? This question is imperative because without truly understanding its motivation, how will our alarms ever be triggered? How will we be able to avoid sin's snares or realize that we are living confined lives? We have a terrible ability to adapt and survive. As Red says in *Shawshank*, "I'm telling you, these walls are funny. First you hate them. Then you get used to them. Enough time passes, it gets so you depend on them. That's institutionalized." We get so used to sin being ever-present and influencing our lives that we forget its presence and even depend on it. *May it never be!*

To understand what motivates sin, we look at the effect it has on us. Jesus teaches in Mark 7:23, "All these evil things come from within, and they defile a person." Sin's work seeks to defile a person. The biblical language of defilement is to make one unclean and thus unworthy to enter into the presence of God (Exodus 29:1–9, 30:17–21, 40:3–32, Psalm 26:6, 73:13). The bigger story is the inability for the unrighteousness of the sin-filled to be in the presence of the righteous God. In other words, sin puts us in an orange jumpsuit and ushers us in to meet with God, only for us to find a plexiglass partition, a metal chair, a black telephone on the wall, and God on the other side with his hand pressed against the glass and his eyes longingly glued on you.

Sin's motivation, its finish line, its end zone is to separate you from God and his Church. Sin is originally and inherently opposed to God; it is entirely evil. In fact, it is the essence and root of all evil. If God is love, it seeks to fill you with hate. If God desires relationship with you, it wants you alone. If God brings the light of hope, it seeks to engulf you in the pit of depression. It is the original enemy of God and seeks to sever every connection God has with his creation, in order to hurt him. As you sit and chat with God about *life on the inside*, sin stands at the door gazing at his watch, waiting to pull you from the room to delight in your brokenness and God's pain. It's not even really about you—sin is first the enemy of God and we are the battlefield. As God is what is best for us, then sin becomes our enemy too.

We need salvation from the isolation of sin. Otherwise, we will spend our lives alone, in the confines of its control. Sin shackles us and leads us into the dark, and we are powerless to leave.

CHAPTER 2

When Lies Are Shackles

Ten years ago, I found myself in a particular cell, shackled by the lies of sin. You couldn't see the walls, but they were there, keeping everyone out—a cell in which I had been imprisoned for 15 years. It was only as my shackles were removed that I realized the lies that sin had told to restrain me. As I poured through scripture, I discovered this was in fact a regular strategy that sin uses to bind and incarcerate us. I found that mine was a typical incarceration for men, shared even by the shepherd King David. In this chapter, we will learn from David's story and expose the three lies sin told him, and LORD willing, find the key to unlock your chains.

LIE 1: YOU ARE IN CONTROL

David's story begins in the middle of his life, in the security of his reign as king over all Israel. It's the story of David and Bathsheba. To many, it may be a familiar story. For those who aren't familiar, you can get the scoop in 2 Samuel chapter 11 in your Bible (or just Google it). If I had to guess, you'd recount the story the following way, even if you know it well: David has an affair with the Hittites' wife, which culminates in murder. With this version, you miss the first lie that sin told David, which happens before the deception and the plotting. It's even before the lust. It happens in the background of verse one. That's the trick of this first lie; it's whispered subtly, where you don't even realize you are buying into it. As soon as you do, it has you. With the decision to buy into the first lie, sin has already locked you up and made you powerless to avoid the second two lies. I tell students all the time, "Be careful about the decisions you make, as they will cause a domino effect on the decisions that come after." If you decide to stay out with your girlfriend way after you should've gone home, the decision to go to her house when everyone is asleep has already been made, and what happens there has already been decided too. The first lie sin tells, that caught David and all of us who stay out when we know we should go home, is *"you are in control."*

In verse 1 of David's story, it says, *"In the spring of the year, the time when kings go out to battle, David sent Joab, and his servants with him, and all Israel. And they ravaged the Ammonites and besieged Rabbah. But David remained at Jerusalem."*[1] David believed the lie that he was in control. It didn't matter what his responsibilities were, and it didn't matter what was best for anyone else. He was king not only of Israel, but his own life, and he could do whatever he wanted.

We all know what it is to be tempted, to want something so deeply that all of our focus is bent on acquiring it. The cravings consume our waking and fleeting thoughts. There are things that capture our attention so completely that our sole focus is to acquire them. Nonetheless, it's not those things that sit on the throne of our hearts. The things are just gifts the *"king"* deserves. The real thing that captures our attention is ourselves, and sin knows it. We want to be king; we want to be in control. Sin doesn't have to put things in front of our face. All it has to do is tell us we deserve to be our own boss, and God is subsequently pushed aside as we sit on the throne. Sin praises our ascent and cries out, "Long live the king!" Then sin, like Grima Wormtongue, whispers all kinds of atrocities in our ear while calling the shots. (Not a *Lord of the Rings* fan? YouTube it.)

This lie is perpetually cropping up in all aspects of our lives, from planning our futures, to picking our entertainment, to the websites and restaurants we visit, to the schedules we keep, and how we manage our finances. Even when planning the most mundane activities, this little lie is lurking in the process. We say, "I will pick you up at seven," and the lie is already believed. You believe you have unilateral control over the future and that you can actually fulfill the promise on your own. With just a quick survey of your life, you will find handfuls of circumstances where you make intentional decisions based purely on the fact that *you* want it that way, regardless of morals or merit. In every single one of those circumstances we, like David, are being bound in chains. Do you remember Veruca Salt from *Willy Wonka and the Chocolate Factory*? "Don't care how, I want it now." You might agree she was a bad egg, but remember what Jesus said when he scribbled in the sand: *"He who is without sin cast the first stone"* (John 8:7). In fact, we seem to behave like all the children invited into the Chocolate Factory. We too are more concerned about ourselves than what's at stake.

When we bite on the lie of control, the jig is up. We are caught and will most likely be hoodwinked by the next two lies as well. The jailor is calling the shots now. So as David lounges around his palace doing whatever seems right, he catches a glimpse of a naked lady. We all know this isn't going to go well.

LIE 2: THERE ARE NO CONSEQUENCES FOR YOUR ACTIONS

"It happened, late one afternoon, when David arose from his couch and was walking on the roof of the king's house, that he saw from the roof a woman bathing; and the woman was very beautiful. And David sent and inquired about the woman. And one said, 'Is not this Bathsheba, the daughter of Eliam, the wife of Uriah the Hittite?'"

—2 Samuel 11:2–3

David has bought into the first lie hook, line, and sinker. In his mind, the right thing to do is to satisfy his desire. He sends servants to bring Bathsheba to the palace, and he has sex with her. It would seem that the decision to sleep with another man's wife should be a troubling and difficult decision...one many suggest they would never make. Even though we all watched the videos about our changing bodies and took ninth grade health class, we are still amazed when someone gets herpes. It seems so logical and obvious that David shouldn't sleep with this woman, but David bought the second lie: "There are no consequences for your actions." This is what happens every time a drunk person gets behind the wheel. Believing they are in control and have the capacity to drive, they fall for the second lie: if they drive, there won't be any consequences. It's not a matter of not considering the consequences, but believing there won't be any. Ten thousand mothers whose children died last year to DUI say otherwise. Are you having trouble relating to this analogy because you've never made the choice to drive drunk? Do you use your phone while you drive? Maybe there are no consequences for your actions either.

Though your experiences might not be as devastating at the onset, consider the loans, the lies, the broken marriages. We make decisions every day based purely on ourselves that have lasting effects in our relationships with strangers and even more often with people we care deeply about who play significant roles in our lives.

LIE 3: NO ONE NEEDS TO KNOW

Well, David bought the lie and he had sex with Bathsheba. After he had been satisfied, like any classy guy, he sends her back home. And guess what? She got pregnant and the next shackles go around his feet. David is stuck with a pregnant woman who is married to another man and a child that he has fathered. He now knows what the consequences are, even though sin promised him there wouldn't be any. He knows they will be devastating and severe, unless he grabs hold of the last lie sin wants him to believe: "No one needs to know." David thinks, "I have to deal with the results of my actions (without consequences for these actions), but I can deal with them myself (control issues) by hiding it from everyone." This lie leads David to deception, abuse, and conspiracy to murder. In fact, when David is pushed to the limit, he writes a letter to Joab instructing him to murder Uriah on the battlefield so no one suspects foul play. David places that letter in the hand of Uriah, looks him in the eye, and sends him back to the front to his doom—all to cover up an illegitimate child from a one-night stand. As this is transpiring, sin is taking David by the chains and leading him deeper and deeper into the darkness. Before, he may have resisted, maybe fought back, but now he walks willingly into his cell so no one will see his chains. The cost of believing sin's lies is a life alone in a dark corner of a large prison. You may prefer the solitude to the shame of being locked up, but we were not made to live alone. David accepted sin's lies: I am in control; there are no consequences for my actions; and no one needs to know.

What he did brought him to the cell next to me, though I didn't recognize him or his situation because I was also in the dark chained by sin. I couldn't see the lies I had accepted just like I couldn't see them on him. We all wind up in this prison locked by sin's shackles in the same way, lost and confused. We think it's better to be in prison than to have everyone know what's happened. (Be careful as you look at your own sin and how you're managing it. You might think you know what you're doing, but in reality you're succumbing to the first lie: you're in control.) At this point in sin's plan, it has accomplished its goal. We are trapped by our own unwillingness to leave. We are separated from the light and life of God and his church. We are separated from the people we love.

CHAPTER 3

The Truth Will Set You Free

I was in my own cell when I met King David. I can tell you this story, not because I am unashamed, but because I know how to deal with sin now. If you don't know how to deal with sin, you will. In sixth grade I was riding the bus, and pictures of naked women were being passed around, some torn from magazines and some drawn. The effects of these images dominated over a decade of my life. Like any one of us who tries to satisfy the Bathsheba effect, I thought that these vices can be picked up and put down on a whim. They can't. Once you wear the shackles, you don't get to decide when you will and won't wear them. They own you, not the other way around. I never thought of the effect it would have on intimacy in my marriage or how it would change the way I saw women. The sex industry turns people into objects for consumption, and sin changes the way we relate to one another. I didn't see women as humans but rather as objects of desire, something to be used and nothing more. I had some marginal peace for a few years by doing everything in my power to avoid sexuality in entertainment, but it wasn't until I had a daughter and found out that almost 90% of women in the sex industry are sexually abused as children that those shackles were finally gone, and I was able to be free from those burdens.[2]

It took the relationship with my precious daughter, and three other women dear to me, to connect an actual person to the figures. The love of Christ was made known to me through those women and is responsible for my redemption. Those relationships account for some of my most cherished faith relationships because of their love. It was through them that Christ removed those shackles from my body and set me free. It still took three more years and another tragedy in my marriage to finally wake me up to what had happened. God showed me the lies sin had told me and at what cost. The love of Christ through these women removed my chains, but I chose to hold on to the last lie of sin, and I stayed in the darkness. With or without shackles, it's still prison. It is so hard to submit to the truth that we are not in control and there are consequences that have to be dealt with. But the hardest thing to admit is that someone has to know.

It was in 2015 that I realized exactly what Paul meant when he wrote, "*Wretched man that I am! Who will deliver me from this body of death?*" (Romans 7:24). In the beginning of that year I found myself begging Jesus for the courage to reach out from the darkness. So, in the back parking lot of Macy's department store, I called my dad. I told him from the beginning everything that happened and about my struggle with addiction, and I openly confessed that I was broken. Then I called my two best friends and my brothers in Christ, and they all said the same thing. They told me Jesus had died to take my sentence and pay for my sins. Sin didn't own me anymore. In other words, they brought the light of Christ into my darkness and released me from it. I tell you these things because chances are you are hiding in the dark too.

THE VICTORY OVER SIN

My story is not unique in any way. Victory over sin is always there. The problem for so many is that they look for it in the wrong places. It was regular practice 50 years ago in fundamentalist churches to fix the sin of homosexuality by remission and public denouncement. A most embarrassing slogan, "Pray the gay away," was a by-product of this sin-inspired teaching. This practice, like so many used in evangelical churches, basically comes down to "just stop sinning," which seems to be built on the premise that the sinner is in control of their sin. Sound familiar!? I'm not trying to comment on the condition of sin; I am speaking to its solution. The solution to sin is not to stop sinning. The solution to sin is Jesus, crucified on my behalf to pay the penalty of my sin and redeem me from it by forgiving me. It's the solution for your sin too, BTW. This is the essence of the Gospel and the foundation of the Church: Jesus' Calvary is the solution to sin.

The only way to abate darkness is to shine the light, and Jesus promises that he will shine through his church. Light isn't afraid of darkness. There has never been a time when darkness was able to snuff out the light. When the light comes, the darkness always recedes, and peace and joy are all that's left. So, I beg you, don't let the darkness hold you for one more second. Reach out to the church, the faith community, and people of God, and with courage lay your sins before the LORD. You will find he is ready and willing to carry them!

If you are questioning the challenge I lay before you, you are probably thinking to yourself, "Why do I have to tell anyone?" Why can't I just confess my sins straight to God? I know, I hear ya, and you can. But are you sure you aren't trying to control the situation, to avoid any consequences like your friends knowing who you really are? Let me just ask: what if God told your pastor and family the sins you confessed and he forgave? Would confessing to God still be such a comfortable option? Or does confessing to God make it so no one needs to know? These are the basic lies, but be sure sin has been telling them for thousands of years and has gotten pretty good at hiding them all over the place. So, when any thought, emotion, intention, or action leaves you feeling distant from others or makes you want to hide, cling to the blood of Jesus and the forgiveness he gave you on the cross, and don't for a moment give sin a foothold. Instead, act by confessing to someone.

"No temptation has overtaken you that is not common to man. God is faithful, and he will not let you be tempted beyond your ability, but with the temptation he will also provide the way of escape, that you may be able to endure it."

—1 Corinthians 10:13

"Is anyone among you sick? Let him call for the elders of the church, and let them pray over him, anointing him with oil in the name of the Lord. And the prayer of faith will save the one who is sick, and the Lord will raise him up. And if he has committed sins, he will be forgiven. Therefore, confess your sins to one another and pray for one another, that you may be healed. The prayer of a righteous person has great power as it is working. Elijah was a man with a nature like ours, and he prayed fervently that it might not rain, and for three years and six months it did not rain on the earth. Then he prayed again, and heaven gave rain, and the earth bore its fruit. My brothers, if anyone among you wanders from the truth and someone brings him back, let him know that whoever brings back a sinner from his wandering will save his soul from

death and will cover a multitude of sins."

—James 5:14–20

TAKEAWAYS

SIN'S GOAL: Sin wants to separate you from God and his Church.

SIN'S TACTICS: Sin tells three lies: You are in control. There are no consequences for your actions. No one needs to know.

GOD'S VICTORY: The solution to sin is not to stop sinning. The solution to sin is Jesus, crucified on your behalf to pay the penalty of your sin and redeem you from it by forgiving you. 2 Corinthians 5:21

ACTION POINT: I beg you, don't let the darkness hold you for one more second. Reach out to the church, the faith community, and with courage lay your sins before Jesus. You will find he is ready and willing to carry them!

CHAPTER 4

Death

THE WOLF

Death is a wolf, like in the old Disney short, *Lambert the Sheepish Lion*. The wolf is always prowling around, looking for an opportunity to devour. In the *Lambert* short, we find the familiar story of a wolf trying to eat sheep. It stalks the flock, lurking in the shadows, and when a sheep separates from the shepherd and his flock, the wolf pounces. It stains the sheep's wool crimson as it drags the sheep into the dark and swallows it up. Like its mother, sin, death has always been the enemy of and innately opposed to God. John 1 calls Jesus' life the origin and spark of life for all mankind. There is no life apart from God's providence, and death is in complete opposition to that life. Jonah describes his "big fish" adventure as a death experience. It isn't one of those "keep away from the light at the end of the tunnel" kind of stories. In chapter two, he pens a Psalm about the event:

"Then Jonah prayed to the LORD *his God from the belly of the fish, saying,*

'I called out to the LORD, *out of my distress, and he answered me; out of the belly of Sheol I cried, and you heard my voice. For you cast me into the deep, into the heart of the seas, and the flood surrounded me; all your waves and your billows passed over me. Then I said, "I am driven away from your sight; yet I shall again look upon your holy temple." The waters closed in over me to take my life; the deep surrounded me; weeds were wrapped about my head at the roots of the mountains. I went down to the land whose bars closed upon me forever; yet you brought up my life from the pit, O* LORD *my God. When my life was fainting away, I remembered the* LORD, *and my prayer came to you, into your holy temple. Those who pay regard to vain idols forsake their hope of steadfast love. But I with the voice of thanksgiving will sacrifice to you; what I have vowed I will pay. Salvation belongs to the* LORD!'

And the LORD *spoke to the fish, and it vomited Jonah out upon the dry land."*

— Jonah 2

Jonah's words depict his experience of being swallowed up by a fish as a terrible fate, likened to being swallowed by death. He speaks of distress, crying, being consumed by waters (the feeling of drowning), being trapped and unable to escape. (Have you ever gone spelunking? To be dozens of feet underground and all of a sudden pinned between rocks, unable to move? That's what Jonah is feeling.) This is where strength and fervor grow faint and life is whisked away. But even in the midst of his terrible fate, Jonah cries out for deliverance to the LORD of salvation and steadfast love. In three days, he is restored to life (albeit in a pile of fishy vomit). Go back and read Jonah's psalm. Try highlighting the parts about death, and then highlight the parts about life with God (yes, that means two colors). Look at the contrast between Jonah's experience with death and his life with God: separation vs. restoration, absence vs. presence, destruction vs. salvation. These contrasts illustrate the battleground between death and God as death tries to finish the job—eternally separating God from his creation.

Jesus' death and resurrection mark the turning of the tide, putting sin and death on their heels. The master plan was destroyed when the tomb was vacated. This means the wolf can no longer wait for the sheep to come to him. He has to switch his strategy to the offensive. In order to capture sheep, he donned a coat of wool and moved into the flock to lower the guard and gain the sheep's trust. In the next three chapters, we will look at the wools the wolf wears. (Say that three times fast.)

CHAPTER 5

Wool Coats

I AM YOUR FRIEND

With my job, I am typically present for milestones in people's lives. I am around for the beginning of family—the birth of children. To be clear, I could barely endure the birth of my own children, so I'm not around for the "main event" so to speak. I prefer to catch up after all the players are in the locker room, washed up, and giving the brief recap. I love being one of the first people invited to the hospital, as every member of the family wonders how they managed to live before this precious new addition came along.

I'm also around for graduations and marriages, when those babies are still freaking out as much as they did in the nursery. I am there to offer an anchor, a physical presence to the faithfulness of God throughout life's journey. In the circle of life, I am there for the last moments and the days after, to help the grieving and the bereaved. I handle the details, big and small, to help families work through the process of loss and assist them as they take new steps into a changed life. Maybe I'm weird, but besides birth and baptism, I prefer funerals over weddings. That's not a commentary on my marriage. Brittany and I have been married since 2010, happily for...hmmm... eight years. (I know she's going to read this.) Anyway, I find funerals to be an important battleground for spiritual warfare because death tries to sneak into the event in tricky ways. I first noticed it when my grandma died.

It was the spring of 2003 when I graduated from Urbandale High School (Go Jayhawks!). After the ceremony, the parents came down for pictures with their graduates and friends. When I met my parents on the gym floor, my mother gave me a hug and said, "Grandma is dying, it's time to go." She had been battling lupus for over 20 years. I was blessed to be the firstborn grandchild, so I was there for some of the good years as she was able to play with me outside, go for walks, and take adventures. By the time my sister showed up four years later, grandma was pretty much restricted to the indoors. We would play games at the table and watch movies in the living room. Although her body was wasting away, her mind stayed sharp. We would talk for hours about everything from the weather to what I wanted to be when I grew up.

The last ten years were rough. Grandpa, born and raised on the family farm (and LORD willing, will die on the family farm), became a full-time caregiver along with his farm duties. The last couple of years, grandma couldn't even lift a spoon, let alone carry out an independent activity.

On the way to the car after graduation, we received the call that she was gone. We went to Fairbank, Iowa, to be with family and have the funeral. Grandpa was broken, but to be honest, so were the rest of us. We walked through the steps and went to the services. Afterwards, we shook hands as everyone in attendance came to pay their respects. Most of them were from the local church. These lifelong farmers and friends would shake my hand and say things like, "She is in a better place." It rubbed me the wrong way, as I was grieving the death of my grandmother. Frankly, I didn't want her in a better place. I wanted her here with me. Other people said, "This is what was best for her." It wasn't what was best for her. It would have been better if she hadn't had lupus at all. But the saying that really made my skin crawl was "At least now her suffering is over." All three of these responses, which I have heard countless times over my career, make it sound as if the person's death is somehow a good thing. You might even be thinking to yourself, "Well yeah, for your grandma it was kind of a good thing because she had suffered so long." But before jumping into condolences, consider the shortest verse in the Bible: *"He wept"* (John 11:35). Jesus, knowing that he would resurrect his friend Lazarus who had died of sickness, still wept when he saw Lazarus' sister Mary because he was deeply moved to mourn with her.[3]

Death made a great strategic move at the resurrection of Jesus. Knowing that it had lost the war and that soon it would be defeated, it subtly moved from opposition to ally. My cousin Jim was an Iowa wrestler throughout high school. Now, for those of you not familiar with the sport or Midwestern traditions, as football is to the South, wrestling is to Iowa. We would close the schools and businesses during the State Wrestling Tournaments. Jim was one of the great high school wrestlers. His father had him wrestling since his first onesie, continually pushing him to be better, to be a champion, and never accept a loss. Their entire family life revolved around wrestling.

At the direction of his father, it consumed Jim's entire life. He won state championships every year of high school while moving up weight classes each year. (BTW, I realize for those who know me, this kind of athletic prowess seems far-fetched; Jim is a distant cousin. So yes, I realize I share no genetic makeup with that part of the family, other than rugged good looks.) Anyway, during his senior year, Jim was offered scholarships to many schools, including a full ride to the University of Iowa. He found himself in the championship match, wrestling an opponent he had barely beaten earlier in the season. Well, this time he lost, and even though the loss seemed small (one loss at State in his entire high school career), Jim never wrestled again. After the match, Jim, his mother, and his sisters were eating lunch together in the cafeteria. When his father approached their table with tray in hand, he looked Jim dead in the face and said, "I don't sit with losers." Then he went over and sat with the boy who had just beaten his son.

I tell you, Jim's dad was like death. He might be sitting at the winners table, but he doesn't belong there; he wasn't invited, and in fact, he is the biggest loser in the room.

In the mind of the Christian, death became the stepping stone or gateway to Heaven. Death suggested, "I am the only way to Heaven so you will have to pass through me, your buddy and pal, in order to get to the good stuff." Search your thoughts on the matter. How often have you considered death as part of life's arc? Always? Do you quote Paul saying, "death isn't bad" because "to die is gain"? It is the normal progression of life that we face death and then eternity. The regularity of death allows it to suggest that it's a good thing, when in truth, it is simply an anticipated thing. Our love of consistency and discomfort with the unexpected makes it seem that the expected death is good because we were counting on it. However, this slight move from enemy to friend makes bereavement a trap for death to ensnare the hopeful.

When death breaks in from the expected "end of life" phase, snatching a cherished one away from us, it reveals the true nature of death. Its disguise is lifted and for a moment our eyes are opened: "What big eyes you have, what big ears you have, what big teeth you have." We see death for what it really is—an enemy.

I have been present for many deaths over the course of my career, but Lily's death stays with me. I officiated the wedding ceremony for Grayson and Kim in April of 2013, a lovely couple excited about their future life together. They had established careers, a home, and in the middle of August would bring home their first child. After the wedding I lost touch with the couple until I got a call one Monday morning. It was Grayson telling me Kim was scheduled to give birth on Wednesday, but in a choked murmur he said, "They did an ultrasound, and there is no heartbeat. Kim is delivering the baby now. Will you please come?" I drove to the hospital and met them in their room located in the delivery wing. The familiar sound of babies crying in the distance gave me a sickening feeling this time because I knew what that sound meant for Grayson and Kim.

Their faces were hollowed out like someone had swallowed their souls. I shook Grayson's hand as I walked in, and I caught eyes with Kim. Her face was puffy from swells of emotion, and she began weeping bitterly. As I moved to give her a hug, I saw Grayson's eyes swell as he turned his face to his shoes and he sat down. They told me her name was Lily and that they would be bringing her in soon. Sitting there in a nursery room with new parents, waiting to hold a cherished new member of the family, the familiarity of the situation raged against my spirit. But when Lily came in the room, it was different. It felt cold and hollow. Grayson walked to the roller crib, and he stood still as a statue staring at his daughter. Kim asked to hold her. She embraced Lily, cooing and rocking her in her arms. I can't tell you how much time passed. I can't count how many pieces of broken hearts were strewn across the floor. I knew in this moment, all hope was gone. Kim offered to let me hold Lily, and I wanted to so desperately. As I held the child, I didn't want to let her go. I held her hand in my hand and looked into her perfect, tiny face with her eyes shut tight and her pursed purple lips and just looked. In those moments, I had a rush of emotion as my crushed spirit was filled with fire like a wild rage that consumed me. Death had done this. My vocabulary shrunk to four letter words as I cursed death for what it had stolen from Lily. I couldn't control the bitter hate that built up inside me from this ancient enemy that just wouldn't give up. I knew I wasn't the only one wrestling with all of these emotions, and I knew what was at stake.

Death had done what it could to Lily, and the target was Grayson and Kim. When anger and rage swells, we look for someone to blame, and here is where death lays the trap. It says, "I'm God's friend, remember? I'm just here helping him out, getting people to Heaven. *If you're going to be mad, be mad at God!*" In a last-ditch effort, it thinks, "If I'm going down, I'm taking God with me." At that point, the anger, like a furnace, hardens the heart against God. This is the crucial moment for us to straighten out what is really going on. Death is our enemy! It doesn't matter if it comes at the end of a twenty-year battle with lupus, or if it comes before birth. Death is the enemy that separates us from the ones we love—God's church. It breaks families and marriages. It wreaks havoc on our values and beliefs. I tell you, every day of your life, curse death for stealing so many loved ones away. Hate its existence and pray, "Come LORD Jesus, and put these things right." Remember that Jesus went to the cross so that this would not be Lily's end. Death wants to separate God from his church, but when Jesus died on the cross and rose from the dead, he won the victory. Though death might separate the church in life, death is temporary, and we are never separated from God. He is present with us in these battles, working for our good in the midst of this terrible shadow.

THE CURSE OF THE COMMONPLACE AND PLEASURE ISLAND

We fear the novel, the unknown, and it makes us uncomfortable and cautious. When our antennas are up, we notice the little things that are out of place—the inconsistencies. Death wants us to be confused and in the dark because that provides it a strategic advantage. So, when we are in unfamiliar territory, we become aware of how our feelings of loss, anger, and confusion don't match up with the standard ideas of, "It's a good thing. Suffering is over," etc. Our awareness removes the sheep's clothing, and death is exposed for the enemy it is. To overcome this weakness, death's best strategy is twofold: for us to think of death as a *normal thing* and for death to control its narrative. First, it wants us to see death as commonplace and regular so that we are so inundated with the idea of death that we don't even notice its presence. It's like the train whistle you noticed every four hours when you first moved into your new place. You wondered how you would ever sleep with its constant cry. By the time you move, you wonder if you will ever sleep without it. Death wants to be so much a part of your life that you believe you can't live without it. This is completely contrary to the hope we have in Jesus' resurrection.

> *"But we see him who for a little while was made lower than the angels, namely Jesus, crowned with glory and honor because of the suffering of death, so that by the grace of God he might taste death for everyone."*

—Hebrews 2:9

The hope in the death of Jesus is that by the grace of God, Jesus has tasted death (died) for everyone. This is what makes his promise so rich with joy and hope. *"Truly, I say to you, there are some standing here who will not taste death until they see the Son of Man coming in his kingdom"* (Matthew 16:28). Just stop for a second. Have you ever considered that death is neither a part of life, nor is it required? Probably not. The saying goes, "Two things are certain in life: death and taxes." On the contrary, it's not certain at all. When Peter searched the tomb and found it empty, we like Peter focused on Jesus' missing body. What we didn't notice was that the absolute presence and authority of death was gone. When Jesus rose, death was disarmed. *"I shall ransom them from the power of Sheol; I shall redeem them from Death. O Death, where are your plagues? O Sheol, where is your sting?"* (Hosea 13:14a). Death wants to become familiar so that the curse of the commonplace pushes us to take it for granted.

Pleasure Island

The second fold (you thought I forgot about the second fold of the twofold plan) is key to the success of the first. Death has to control the narrative—the relationship. It will be familiar and consistently present in your life, but it will cover its true nature in another wool coat to confuse you about its true intent.

The first time we came to Reno was in the spring of 2015. I was ministering in Valdosta, Georgia, at the time and was extended a call to serve at St. Luke's. We came to visit to get to know the area, the people, and the faith community at St. Luke's. It was a great trip that God used to confirm for us that he was calling us to serve in the "Biggest Little City in the World." During that visit, the church put us up in a local hotel casino. At that point in my life, I had never been in a casino, so it was an unfamiliar experience. I was alert to the inconsistencies the casino floor presented.

To give you a little back story, my mother loves pizza. Actually, "loves" is an understatement. If Jacob had offered her pizza, she would have given him her birthright, and maybe even her firstborn. So while I was growing up, the Hut was a regular dinner out for the family. If you remember Pizza Hut from the late 80s and early 90s, they always had a Mario Brothers video game. It cost a quarter and every time we went (which was often), I would ask Dad if I could play, and his response *every single time* was "That's a waste of money."

That's the mentality I was raised on, which I brought into the casino with me: these "games" are a waste of money. Every casino floor had billions of twinkly lights and thousands of colors and sounds, and there were all kinds of activities with people bustling about. It was so in-your-face it reminded me of the "It's a Small World" ride in Disneyland. (By the way, you might love "It's a Small World." That's what the designers of the ride intended. I'm guessing the designers of the casino had the same goal in mind.) I thought to myself, "This looks like it's *supposed to* be lots of fun."

During our visit, we would come back to the casino in the afternoons, exhausted from the day's events. Passing through the casino floor on the way to the elevators made me uncomfortable. I knew it was a waste of money, but it seemed to be trying to convince me that this was the happiest place on earth. There wasn't even a clock in the whole place because, like Pleasure Island in Disney's *Pinocchio*, something else was happening behind the lights. Coming to Reno from the East Coast messed with our internal body clock. Brittany and I would be wide awake at 4:00 a.m., so we took the extra time to explore the city. As we made our way through the casino to the rental car, the floor told a very different story at four in the morning. The lights, the sounds, the colors, and the bar were still open, but the people weren't having fun. We saw people sleeping on slot machines, slumped over in chairs. We watched as one man threw a glass in the hallway, scattering shards across the floor as he crumpled into a heap on the ground. The casino tells a very different story on the floor than the story of the people trapped there. In order to become your friend, someone you enjoy, death presents itself as the place where dreams come true.

Horror Movies Make a Killing

Bad joke, but it's true. In 2015, the industry made $1.6 billion in profits. Today the annual cost to produce these films is around $300 million, which makes them the cheapest movies to produce with the highest profit margins. Horror movies were the profit stars of 2017 as well. The remake of "*It*" made over $700 million in 2017, and it only cost $35 million to produce. I despise horror films because of the effect they have on me when I'm alone in the dark. Specifically, when I'm in the wilderness hunting. Yes, I'm a big baby, and no, I can't handle how my mind wanders while I stare into the darkness outside my tent in the middle of nowhere. I had to do research to understand why horror films are so popular with other people. I found an article on thedailybeast. com, written by Sharon Begley, called, "Why Our Brains Love Horror Movies: Fear, Catharsis, a Sense of Doom." Begley interviewed a former professor of psychology who said horror movies offer the viewer the thrills of terror, with no risk. He says, "We know that in an hour or two, we're going to walk out whole...We're not going to have any holes in our head, and our hearts will still be in our bodies." This is a deadly trick. Death pulls the wool over our eyes in this illogical conclusion. We think that the effect of the things we see won't follow us out of the theater and they won't change the way we see our world. As I illustrated with sin, this is a lie that allows the enemy inside our minds and hearts. It changes our perspective and colors our perception.

In horror movies, death is creating a two-faced facade: First, the death you see on screen has no effect on your life; and second, death can give you thrills and a flood of emotions that are enjoyable and otherwise absent from your mundane life. Horror connoisseurs will use this genre as a way to fill a void in their regular lives. For a couple of hours they engage their senses and emotions in a roller coaster of experience. It's thought to be a secure way to seek thrills (at least more secure than skydiving or something else equally crazy). But what it does is desensitize us to what death is actually doing. With all the blood and guts, the suspense and the pursuit thrown in, when the final axe comes down we don't even notice death because we already got our high. Death is the curtain call, like a bow to the greatest showman. It offers us the bump we are seeking. When a car accident occurs, even with a fender bender, it slows traffic down to a crawl. After the vehicles are out of the way, people move slowly not to stay safe but to take a look to see what's happened for themselves. When the wreck is really bad, your emotions rise as you slowly drive by to see the mangled metal of what might have been a car, and your mind speculates about the people who were once inside the vehicle. Test your feelings. Do you take the same delight when watching a horror flick? Or does what you see on screen feel different from who is in the ambulance or under the blanket lying on the road? Something doesn't add up. Do you see how death suggests it's something different because it's on screen instead of on pavement? That's death's trick.

Collateral Damage and Call of Duty

By now you've probably figured out that horror films are not my thing. Maybe they're not yours either. I like superhero movies. Without getting into why *Batman* is far superior to *Spiderman*, allow me to explain my fascination (he is way better by the way.) I have always been a fan of trilogies: *Star Wars, Indiana Jones, Back to the Future, Lord of the Rings, the Matrix* (just kidding I only like the first one). I love that they take the story further. I love digging deeper into the narrative, exploring the characters and their world. Marvel has pushed the envelope to the max, making 22 interlacing movies since 2007. They have become the only genre I will go to the theater to watch. On May 6, 2016, the third installment of *Captain America* came out, subtitled, *Civil War*. The heroes in the film battle each other because of a divide caused by alliances and the changing status quo.

For 12 movies, we had seen these heroes save the world (sometimes universe) from catastrophe and devastation. We were thrilled and wowed by the strength of their powers, integrity, and spirit. We cherished the friendships, the bonds, even the villains who brought this gladiatorial event to our arena. But the thirteenth installment, *Civil War*, asks the question none of us asked: What about everyone else on screen? The governments of the world ask our heroes, "What about the collateral damage caused by your epic fights?" This forces the question of governance for the Avengers, which results in the dissolution of the team.

Earth is now vulnerable and so are we. All this time watching this saga unfold, we realize that we never asked the question "What about all of those other people?" They are called extras, simply put on screen to be ignored where death plays another trick. Death is not worth noticing. It is so prevalent and so familiar that you don't even need to pay attention to its presence. In the show *The Office*, Toby Flenderson constantly warns Michael Scott about black mold and asbestos, saying, "We should really have the office air quality tested—these are silent killers." Scott replies, "You are the silent killer. Go back to the Annex." Like Michael Scott, we shrug off any acknowledgement of an issue as not worth our attention.

Herein death hides its cost in the greater purpose of the story with its devastating impact in grand display. Have you ever counted the people who die while *Saving Private Ryan*? You're not supposed to. It's just part of the nature of a war movie. Death is present, familiar, and expected. Death goes unnoticed and unaccounted for, so we think it's just another mundane part of the greater story of our lives.

The same lie is verbosely told in video games. I am part of the Mario generation (even though my dad tried to ruin my childhood by expecting me to play without a screen). In high school, I got a Nintendo 64 and played *Goldeneye*, a first person shooter, which means the point of the game is to shoot people. In college, it was *Halo on* Xbox, and in seminary I grew into *Call of Duty* on PlayStation. Following the same hoax, I never added up my death toll on any of these games, let alone the sum total of all of them. In my current game, I killed 30,000, so my total would be somewhere around 500,000 on a conservative estimate.

The current rendition is on PS4 where I play *Call of Duty, WWII* *with* a church planter, a high school chaplain, a missionary to Australia, and a few friends from my church. The graphics are detailed, crisp, and astounding. We play-fight in the French town of Carentan, which looks exactly like it did in the 1940s. The guns we use are all from the period and look historically accurate to the detail. One of the most troubling weapons is the flamethrower that lights the enemy on fire, and they wail and scream when hit. Even in the middle of a game, the sound is troubling. Despite having heard it hundreds of times, it still sends a chill down my spine. Games have gotten very realistic.

The first time I played the Normandy map, I was shocked at how real it looked and felt. It took me back to 2002 when I stepped off the bus at the American Cemetery and Memorial at Normandy. Walking through rows and rows of white crosses and stars, I was reminded of the cost men paid on that soil to free Europe. It was a hallowed honor to stand where these men had given their lives. At the edge of the grounds, the cliff that lined Omaha beach was in full view, and it still showed hedgehogs anchored in the waters that once ran red. It was a sobering experience. How present was the history of their sacrifice when death stole the lives of so many courageous men.

When I first played the game, it all came flooding back, and I was filled with deep emotion and respect for those men. I also felt embarrassment for the game I was playing that cost them so much. Since that time, I have played the Normandy map dozens of times, and the feeling is lost in the game. How fast can I climb the beach? How many times will I die and restart before we win? The concerns of the competition wipe away any thought of the cost, and death gives a knowing wink.

What You Use for Entertainment Changes You

The shows we watch, the games we play, and the things we use for entertainment all have an impact on us. They don't just stop when we turn them off. Law enforcement and military institutions use game-like simulations to desensitize people to death. There's been tons of research done to link video games like *Doom* and *Grand Theft Auto* to the shooting strategies of Klebold and Harris in the Columbine High School tragedy of 1999. The truth is that what we put into our eyes, minds, and hearts has a lasting effect on us. Death doesn't want you to know this truth. Instead, it uses your ignorance and lack of attention to get close and personal to change the way you think about death.

For All You Robinson Crusoe Types

You might be an avid opposer to video games and on-screen entertainment, thinking, "We didn't need that stuff when I was a kid." Unfortunately, death's ploy through entertainment is as old as the hills and has been seen in all art forms. The poem by Henry Scott-Holland, a priest at St. Paul's Cathedral of London, is a regular at funerals. It's titled, "Death is Nothing at All." Google it.

I hope by now words like Scott-Holland's cut deep against your perception. No matter the intent of the poem, would you put this in the hands of Grayson and Kim to offer a thought about Lily's death? How about the mothers whose sons died on D-Day? I'm guessing not, because you and I both know it's full of fake news.

In the seventh installment of my absolute favorite series, *Harry Potter*, Hermione is given a copy of *The Tales of Beedle the Bard*. It's a set of short stories that includes *The Tale of the Three Brothers*. In the story, death meets the brothers and tricks two of the them. Death's treachery results in murder and suicide for those brothers. The youngest brother hides from death, and when it's time to die (as if death is a requirement), he allows death to find him. The story finishes like this: "It was only when the third brother reached a great age, he took off the Cloak of Invisibility and gave it to his son. Greeting Death *as an old friend*, they departed this life as equals." Through entertainment, death makes tiny suggestions to bring you in close and change the circumstance. Death is neither a friend, nor an equal. You are set for life everlasting with the One Jesus, who conquered death on your behalf.

IT'S NOT REAL SO IT DOESN'T MATTER

The hinge pin to death's entertainment strategy is suggesting that it's not real. That way, it can be whatever it wants to be. Let's process. How many deaths do you think we have seen on the silver screen? How many on television? Millions? Yet in the name of entertainment, in all hosts of gruesome and novel ways, the idea of millions of people dead by explosions, knives, catastrophes, battles, and unrelenting killers goes unnoticed. Do you feel the same way about the deaths of 500,000 in the Nazi Holocaust? Should they be noticed? What about in books and other physical print? What about the Internet? Can you even call to mind any instances? Is it even worth it to try? Do you feel the same way about the deaths of nearly 1,000,000 Tutsi men, women, and children who were killed with clubs and rocks in 1994? The death toll I have amassed on *Call of Duty* with no concern and barely a blink of an eye rivals the children lost to abortion in the last century. Is their death of any concern? Does it cause me to blink? When we unmask death from the shroud of entertainment, it becomes clear that this deep evil has been hanging around far too close and far too long without notice or care. It's time to put it in its place.

I AM YOUR RELEASE/ESCAPE

The last trick is the worst. It preys on the vulnerable and marginalized. When sin attacks on all fronts, it will use others' influences on our lives, or it will come from within us with lies of no value and minimal worth. Like the ol' good cop, bad cop routine, sin plays the bad cop, isolating us and drawing out deep feelings of abandonment, a lack of self-worth, and/or paralysis. The constant onslaught of emotions like waves in the rising tide can be suffocating. Then death slides in with the good cop bit, presenting itself as a friend, but all the while with your worst interest in mind. It offers despair as hope, confinement as a way out, and death as the release. It preys on the fight-or-flight mechanisms woven into our survival instincts to motivate us to unreasonable action.

This is a serious problem in the United States. Researchers estimate 9.6 million people have experienced suicidal ideation.[4] From 2012 to 2017, the number of youth under 18 who experience severe depression increased from 5.9% to 8.2%, and 1.7 million of those youth did not receive treatment. That's enough to fill every Major League Baseball stadium in the country and still have half a million without a seat. Recall sin's goal—to separate you from God and his church. Isolation is the name of the game. You can see how depression can be a powerful tool for sin. *To be clear*: I am *not saying* experiencing depression is sin. I am saying that sin can trigger depression and use the condition as a circumstance and opportunity to isolate you. This chapter isn't a self-help guide or road map for coping with depression. As I stated in the chapter dealing with sin, when you are feeling pressure to isolate yourself, the best thing is to connect. So, if you are experiencing depression of any kind, my recommendation is to reach out to a support network, whether it's a group, a coach, or a professional counselor. They can support you with the specific circumstances you are facing. Just remember, it's okay to struggle. Jesus promises to be with you through it and so does his

Church. Sometimes death will play the good cop and offer its help as your *only way* out, but that is a lie.

Netflix produced a miniseries in 2017 called *13 Reasons Why*. It's the story of Clay Jensen, a high school student who receives a mysterious box of cassettes with audio recordings from Hannah Baker, a classmate. They chronicle the conditions and experiences that led her to suicide two weeks prior. Thirteen episodes retell the stories on the tapes that include the continuous demoralizing circumstances of her life. If you haven't seen the series, be careful before you dive in. As I mentioned earlier, what we watch has an effect on us. My wife blames that miniseries for the depressive haze that seemed to hover over our house the weeks during and after our watching it. However, I do believe that it can be useful to watch it with the lens of understanding, in order to learn how sin and death regularly work in our relationships. When watching it, try to point out the sin in each episode, including the actions as well as who it affects. Take note of where the beliefs and values of the individual originate and how they spread and affect others. Notice the drastic changes in Hannah's personality, relationships, outlook, and even her appearance as she tries to cope with sin's onslaught. By the end of her story, her life is so consumed with sin (mostly from outside herself in the actions of others) that living seems a worse alternative than death.

Often in the confusion of loss and grief, logic is clouded and emotions swell, engulfing all reason. There is the lie: *that death is an escape from the tragedy of life.* This is the opposite of the truth! *"Then desire when it has conceived gives birth to sin, and sin when it is fully grown brings forth death"* (James 1:15). The truth is that death is the culmination of sin, not the escape from it. In other words, death is the consequence of sin, not the release from it. Romans 6:23a says, *"For the wages of sin is death."*

Time for a reality check for all of us sheep. Jesus, in his parable about the Noble Shepherd in John 10, illuminates the truth that opposes death's lie. In his parable, he calls the sin-inspired leadership "thieves."[5] Even though Jesus is describing those who governed God's people throughout the generations, take a look deeper to recognize that sin, death, and the devil worked in and through those individuals who did terrible things. He compels us to listen to his voice in the daily matter of our lives and to recognize his ways in contrast to the thieves. He is open and direct—transparent. Thieves sneak in and try to use underhanded opportunities to dominate. The shepherd leads the sheep, whereas the thief spurs them.

"The thief comes only to steal and kill and destroy" (John 10:10a). The truth is, sin and death seek only to steal, kill, and destroy your hope, your joy, your relationships, and your very lives. Their aspirations are similar to Lucifer, the thief mentioned here. Watch the last episode of *13 Reasons Why* and see what Hannah's death does to her and to everyone around her. It doesn't release anyone from anything. In fact, it claims another victim. No one escapes the consequences of their sin. In reality, her death ensnares them in their guilt without resolve. *It removes every opportunity to apply the solution to their sin, which is forgiveness.* Has death made her any less alone? Has it removed the effects of sin in any way? It seems only to have completed its work.

In John 10:10, Jesus finishes, *"The thief comes only to steal and kill, and destroy; I came that they may have life and have it abundantly."* Jesus has come that you may have life, true life in liberty, and to the full— not without suffering, and not without joy. His ministry, set before the foundation of the world, is to accomplish this task: to bring true life, washed clean of sin and death, to heal the deepest wounds of our broken relationships, and to make our splintered lives whole. How does he accomplish this task? Jesus says, *"I am the good shepherd. The good shepherd lays down his life for the sheep."* To this point, if your journey is bringing you through the valley of the shadow of death, you might be feeling like we have only described the water you're drowning in. Please know you are not alone, and no matter your life circumstances, there is always an opportunity for relief within the Church community. He has given this life-guarding ministry to the Church to encourage one another, to build each other up, and to provide a way out. *"No temptation has overtaken you that is not common to man. God is faithful, and he will not let you be tempted beyond your ability, but with the temptation he will also provide the way of escape, that you may be able to endure it"* (1 Corinthians 10:13). The faith community is the way of escape and supports you in all those moments and seasons of your life. So allow me to throw you a life jacket.

CHAPTER 6

The Victory over Death

"But in fact Christ has been raised from the dead, the first fruits of those who have fallen asleep. For as by a man came death, by a man has come also the resurrection of the dead. For as in Adam all die, so also in Christ shall all be made alive. But each in his own order: Christ the first fruits, then at his coming those who belong to Christ. Then comes the end, when he delivers the kingdom to God the Father after destroying every rule and every authority and power. For he must reign until he has put all his enemies under his feet. The last enemy to be destroyed is death."

—1 Corinthians 15:20–26

Paul is known to pack a lot of theology into a little package. Here in just six verses, Paul outlines the war that death wages against our lives to teach the Christians in Corinth how the resurrection of Jesus Christ has changed the direction of life. He starts at the beginning of the arc with Adam and the fall into sin in Genesis chapter 3. Paul refers to death's origin through a man (Adam): *"Therefore, just as sin came into the world through one man, and death through sin, and so death spread to all men because all sinned"* (Romans 5:12). Paul is referring to Adam in Genesis chapters 1–4, specifically what happens in chapter 3. It was through Adam and Eve's temptation that sin was born, and when sin matures, death is the result.[6] Death has ruled in creation since Adam, and the death toll continues to rise, generation after generation, as children are born into and die in sin. Paul is excited because while death ruled in the world for thousands of years, he says, *"in the same way one man brought death, so a man has come and through his resurrection has brought life for all creation"* (1 Corinthians 15:21). Then Paul foreshadows the end of this story arc as Jesus ultimately removes death's control over creation. First was the resurrection of Jesus, the firm sign that he has defeated sin, death, and the devil. Second will be the return of Jesus where all those of the faith will be with him forever (cue the end of time moment when the trumpets sound and Jesus returns in glory! Oh what valor!). And finally at the end, he will destroy all enemies of the Kingdom of God: sin, Satan (that ancient serpent), and lastly, death.

Jesus' death and resurrection are only beneficial to us because of a key component in his ministry: his humanity (Galatians 4:4–7). In order to defeat death for us, he had to *be one* of us. He had to be perishable as we are perishable. He had to live our existence and experiences. The good news is he was able to accomplish this in every respect as a human, just as we are human, yet without falling into sin as we do. If you find yourself drowning in the shadow of death, remember that Jesus was born of Mary to sympathize with your circumstance. He knows what it feels like to be abandoned by your friends (Mark 14:50), to be cursed by others' sin (Galatians 3:13), and to anguish in the shadow of death (Luke 22:44). Through all of it, he makes this promise to you, even in the face of his own death: *"I will never leave you nor forsake you"* (Deuteronomy 31:6). You will never be alone. Death will not win.

Death is the final enemy of God's creation; the nail in the coffin, the relay anchor, so to speak, in sin's plan to separate God from his Church. Death intended to be infinitely permanent—the complete separation from God. But Jesus went behind enemy lines, relinquishing his own life into the tomb through death. He then opened the door from the inside out so that death could no longer hold its inhabitants.

> *"For this perishable body must put on the imperishable, and this mortal body must put on immortality. When the perishable puts on the imperishable, and the mortal puts on immortality, then shall come to pass the saying that is written: 'Death is swallowed up in victory.' 'O death, where is your victory? O death, where is your sting?' The sting of death is sin, and the power of sin is the law. But thanks be to God, who gives us the victory through our Lord Jesus Christ."*
>
> —I Corinthians 15:53–56

The once dead, now living Jesus removes the now finite weapon of death. Death was eternal, now no longer. So what can death threaten us with? Our Lord Jesus has made it subservient to his will. It too has bent its knee to the majesty of the Lamb.

THE NOW AND NOT YET

Now, 2,000 years after the resurrection and victory over death, we live in the "now and not yet." This is a contrast that confuses and offers easy prey for the enemy, but with clarity brings encouragement for the day and hope for tomorrow. When Jesus rose from the dead, his resurrection defeated death. Death is still with us in the now. When Jesus comes again, death will be abolished forever, and that is the hope we have in the not yet.

When grappling with any question about death, we need to apply the experience of now and the hope of not yet. For example, Jesus' victory over death is now. We live our lives within the truth that death is not able to remove us from God or our loved ones. It allows us to follow Jesus in sacrificial living. It enables us to offer our lives for the greatest cause—*"Greater love has no one than this, that someone lay down his life for his friends"* (John 15:13). But that victory is also in the not yet. Death is still a present reality in our journey. It is still capable of bringing temporal separation from our loved ones, with griefs and pains almost unbearable. To the now of Jesus' victory, we cry out with the hosts of Heaven, *"Worthy is the Lamb who was slain, to receive power and wealth and wisdom and might and honor and glory and blessing!"* (Revelation 5:12). To the not yet of Jesus' victory, we cry with the Church triumphant, *"How long before you will judge and avenge our blood on those who dwell on the earth?"* (Revelation 6:10).

So, when you approach the bereaved at a funeral to offer condolences and wonder what to say, consider the now and the not yet, as their experience contains both. Offer a word from each. Ask yourself, what are they processing in that moment? There will be a spectrum of thoughts and emotions that are difficult to separate. They may be despairing, hurting, angry, or confused at the change in relationship with their lost one. Affirm their feelings and point to the cause: "I am so sorry; death has taken him/her from you." Speak to the hope of the resurrection, to their joy and jubilance at the victory Jesus won on their loved ones' behalf. If they aren't ready for the not yet because they are experiencing the hardship of the now, sometimes just the love in a hug is enough affirmation for the hope in the not yet.

SEEING DEATH THROUGH TWO LENSES: LAW AND GOSPEL

As Christians, we are particularly vulnerable to the schemes of death because we are always living in two realities. We are sinners, completely incapable of doing what's right, and yet saints who are washed clean of the stains of sin and made right by the Holy Spirit in Christ Jesus. We are alive in the Gospel, the death, and the resurrection of Jesus. We are dead by the commands of God in his Law. We see death from both of these lenses. We celebrate a day we call "Good Friday" (not to be confused with "Black Friday" in November). Good Friday is the day we remember the death of Jesus, which reversed the very current of all created life. We remember it as "good" because of what it accomplished on our behalf. We see it through the Gospel, yet in view of the Law, it is the most awful, unjust death in the history of the world. Nothing could make any less sense. Nothing could ever be more terrible than the death of Jesus.

It will be one of your lifelong pursuits to see life and death through both Law and Gospel in order to put all thoughts and emotions where they belong. You need to be able to make the distinction between the hope we have through Jesus in the midst of death, without confusing death's opposition to that hope in the situation. You need to seal your heart and the heart of others in the faithful promise of the resurrection and allow grieving emotions and thoughts their true expression against sin and death. You need to rightly handle this distinction with the ability to proclaim the hope of Jesus in the face of our enemies, locking them into their cages and keeping them from wreaking havoc on the lives of those involved. The last half of this book will teach you how these tools work, and how to find a community to help you employ them.

TAKEAWAYS

DEATH'S GOAL: Death wants to separate you from God and his Church *eternally*.

DEATH'S TACTICS: Death wants to be overlooked.
Death wants you to believe it's a normal part of life.
Death wants you to blame God for a loved one's death.
Death wants you to believe it's a good thing, the release from suffering.
Death presents itself as entertaining, so common you don't notice.
Death presents itself as an escape.

GOD'S VICTORY: Death is not a friend. You are destined for life everlasting with the One Jesus who conquered death on your behalf.

CHAPTER 7

Devil

THE GREAT AND POWERFUL OZ

The person and character of the devil holds mythical notions in the minds of most Christians and even more so outside of the Church. Some will think of the devil as the yin to God's yang. To be clear, the devil is not on par with the LORD. He is a created being, not holding the attributes of God. He is neither omniscient, nor omnipresent. To this point, he is not omnipotent either. He is of single being and limited understanding. He has the same chance of victory over Jesus as I do with striking out Ted Williams, arguably the best hitter in MLB history. To understand that ancient enemy, that serpent who is the devil, we have to understand his story.

TRIUNE GOD AND THE DIVINE COUNCIL

"God has taken his place in the divine council; in the midst of the gods he holds judgment"

—Psalm 82:1

"Let's start at the very beginning. A very good place to start. When you read, you begin with ABC. When you sing, you begin with Do, Re, Mi"—Maria, *Sound of Music*. When we unpack the devil's story, we must start at the beginning, which does not begin with the devil. If it did, it would change the entire creation paradigm because it would no longer be good. Like every story, it begins with God and his character. Genesis 1 and 2 set the tone for the first five books of the Bible and confirm base truths of God's character. First and foremost, the recurring theme of the Creation stories is "good." Creation is a reflection of God's goodness. This simple fundamental truth inspires childlike comfort in his works and ways because from his goodness flows life for all created things, love for his creation, and grace which provides the means for his continued favor. All of this boils down to one simple truth—The Alpha and Omega, Ancient of Days, I AM that I AM is relational and wants to be in relationship with his creation. He allows himself to be impacted by us, our lives, and our actions. He expresses sympathy (Exodus 3:7–8), anger (Psalm 7:11), laughter (Psalm 37:13), grief (Genesis 6:6), love (1 John 4:8), jealousy (Joshua 24:19), and joy (Zechariah 3:17). He responds to circumstances as minute as the daily happenings of a person's life and as wide reaching as the cosmos. In fact, he is so relational that he invites his creation to be involved in his creative work. Look at the call to Adam in Eden. God invited Adam to name all the creatures. God brought them to Adam and included him in his creative work. We also see another faction of created beings brought into God's work in Genesis 1:26: *"Then God said, 'Let us make man in our image, after our likeness.'"* Many people point to the first person plurals in this statement as evidence of the Trinity in the Old Testament. While it is true that the Trinity can be implied by "us" and "our," it is not the referent in Moses' mind. Psalm 82:1 gives the name for the "us" and "our," calling it the divine council.

To help me understand the concept, I picture King Arthur and the Knights of the Round Table. King Arthur built a round table where he invited his knights to sit. He pointed out that there was no head and no foot. Everyone was equal at this table. King Arthur was welcoming his subjects to be involved in his decision-making process during his rule of Camelot. But make no mistake, no one at the table questioned who the king was. The point the king was making is a relational one. This is how I see the divine council. God is god and needs no other input in his workings. However, his desire to relate with his creation moves him to welcome certain creatures into his decision making. If you're worried about the sovereignty of God at this notion, chill. Arguably, his ability to work out all things according to his will, *while* welcoming input, only raises our view of his sovereignty. There are lots of references and narratives of the divine council's work throughout scripture, but that's for another book. To keep it simple, on this council, at the right and left hands of the Father sit the Son and the Holy Spirit. At this table, you will also find prophets, priests, kings, angels/servants, and Lucifer.

LUCIFER'S ORIGIN

To protect the goodness of God, some have suggested that God didn't create the devil. Instead they suggest that he was an entity in opposition to God, whose origin was some kind of balancing like yin and yang or the Force. In a reversed statement from Supreme Leader Snoke, "The light rises and the dark to meet it." The biblical narrative opposes all of these concepts and has a very different depiction of the devil's creation and purpose. In fact, though the name "Lucifer" doesn't show up in the Bible, it is taken from the Hebrew *helel* which literally means "shining one." It's the Hebrew in Isaiah 14:12 *"O Day Star."* In Ezekiel 28 the prophet laments over the King of Tyre who is submitting himself to the devil's will. In verse 12, the prophet's word turns towards the devil specifically:

> *"...Thus says the LORD God: 'You were the signet of perfection, full of wisdom and perfect in beauty. You were in Eden, the garden of God; every precious stone was your covering, sardius, topaz, and diamond, beryl, onyx, and jasper, sapphire, emerald, and carbuncle; and crafted in gold were your settings and your engravings. On the day that you were created they were prepared. You were an anointed guardian cherub. I placed you; you were on the holy mountain of God; in the midst of the stones of fire you walked. You were blameless in your ways from the day you were created.'"*

—Ezekiel 28:12–19

Though some of these lines are difficult to translate because they are not mirrored in many Hebrew texts, the context is clear. Lucifer was the first in glory of all creation, God's number two. He was the pinnacle reflection of the glory of God, filled with wisdom and perfect beauty. All the beautiful and precious stones of the ancient world used for the finest ornamentation were prepared for Lucifer's adornment. He was created to be an anointed guardian cherub. Cherubs are the creatures given to anoint (cover) the articles of the Covenant in the Holy of Holies (Exodus 25:19–20, 1 Kings 6:24, Hebrews 9:5). Their wings are spread over the articles as a sign of humility because even though these items were holy to the people, they were still only the footstool of the glory of God, a reflection of his glory in Heaven. These creatures maintain the humility of God's people and creation before God, a sign of the humbleness of creation. The heavenly beings that appear as a lion, ox, man, and eagle with similar wings and responsibilities as depicted in Revelation and Ezekiel might share the same purpose as the cherub on Earth. Cherubs act as mediators for God's people, and Ezekiel says Lucifer was anointed *guardian* cherub. The guardian's responsibility is maintaining security, like a gun safe. The guardian acts as a covering and is there to keep the kids from access and potential abuse. Lucifer was established to be the mediator who maintained humility for God's people and limited access to the Holiness of God. In this role he takes on another title: the Accuser.

LUCIFER'S ROLE ON THE DIVINE COUNCIL

"A Vision of Joshua the High Priest: Then he showed me Joshua the high priest standing before the angel of the LORD, and Satan standing at his right hand to accuse him."

—Zechariah 3:11

"And I heard a loud voice in heaven, saying, 'Now the salvation and the power and the kingdom of our God and the authority of his Christ have come, for the accuser of our brothers has been thrown down, who accuses them day and night before our God.'"

—Revelation 12:10

As God's number two, Lucifer sets the bar for relating to God. In the splendor of his created attributes he cherishes God's holiness above all other creatures. Lucifer's position on the divine council as depicted in Zechariah 3:11 and Revelation 12:10 is to sit next to the Father and accuse all creation of being unworthy of his Holiness. To witness such a verbal debate, see Job 1–3. In short, Lucifer's role has been to constantly bring to light all of humanity's shortcomings. As we see in the Garden of Eden, Lucifer's zealous temptation of Eve and Adam resulted in the fruition of their faithlessness and the origin of sin.

Ezekiel depicts the Genesis 3 event from the heavenly realms in chapter 28:

> *"...till unrighteousness was found in you. In the abundance of your trade you were filled with violence in your midst, and you sinned; so I cast you as a profane thing from the mountain of God, and I destroyed you, O guardian cherub, from the midst of the stones of fire. Your heart was proud because of your beauty; you corrupted your wisdom for the sake of your splendor. I cast you to the ground; I exposed you before kings, to feast their eyes on you. By the multitude of your iniquities, in the unrighteousness of your trade you profaned your sanctuaries; so I brought fire out from your midst; it consumed you, and I turned you to ashes on the earth in the sight of all who saw you. All who know you among the peoples are appalled at you; you have come to a dreadful end and shall be no more forever."*

> —Ezekiel 28:15b–19

Lucifer's zeal and desire for the righteousness of God moved him outside of the will of God. Instead of guarding the glory of God, he moved God's people to sin in the epitome of the saying, "the ends do not justify the means." Lucifer's wisdom and beauty were corrupted by his own desire for the glory of God and willingness to sacrifice humanity on his behalf. Because of this, he was found profane and sinful and was no longer welcome in the expressed will and presence of God. But the job to guard the Holiness of God was vacant, like Lancelot's seat at the Round Table, so he still maintained the role of accuser and from earth would continue to dominate humanity by tempting them into sin— until the day God sent his Son to be born of Mary. Jesus was born under the Law and under the cherubim, to redeem those standing accused of no righteousness of their own.

When Jesus became the propitiation for our sin and rose from the dead, he accomplished a righteousness and holiness, unburdened and untarnished, that ensured our access to God. As Jesus ascended to Heaven, we see the depiction of his entry into the presence of God in Revelation 5. No one was worthy in Heaven or earth to open the scroll which brings the end of redemptive history, but by his death and resurrection he had accomplished our Holiness, and as he sits at the right hand of the Father, he brings us into the divine council. At his coronation, the final judgment of Satan will occur, for by the blood of Jesus' sacrifice there is no place for an accuser in the presence of God because we are redeemed!

> *"And the great dragon was thrown down, that ancient serpent, who is called the devil and Satan, the deceiver of the whole world— he was thrown down to the earth, and his angels were thrown down with him. And I heard a loud voice in heaven, saying, 'Now the salvation and the power and the kingdom of our God and the authority of his Christ have come, for the accuser of our brothers has been thrown down, who accuses them day and night before our God. And they have conquered him by the blood of the Lamb and by the word of their testimony, for they loved not their lives even unto death. Therefore, rejoice, O heavens and you who dwell in them! But woe to you, O earth and sea, for the devil has come down to you in great wrath, because he knows that his time is short!'"*

—Revelation 12:9–12

LUCIFER'S MOTIVATION

Every hero (and even anti-hero in this case) needs an origin story. It lays the groundwork and helps us comprehend what's coming in the sequel; it establishes a powerful motivation, something that moves the character into action against all odds. This is most certainly true of Satan. This question arises often: "Why does Satan keep trying, even though he has already lost? Has he not read Revelation!?" The root question here is, "What could be so motivating to move Satan to try, even in the face of certain failure?" Why does he keep working against God's people when we know that no one can separate us from the faith of Christ?

"My sheep hear my voice, and I know them, and they follow me. I give them eternal life, and they will never perish, and no one will snatch them out of my hand. My Father, who has given them to me, is greater than all, and no one is able to snatch them out of the Father's hand. I and the Father are one."

—John 10:25–30

This is where ignorance in understanding Satan's motivation becomes a pivotal tool in his arsenal. In *The Art of War*, Sun Tzu says, "The whole secret lies in confusing the enemy, so that he cannot fathom our real intent." Satan takes confusion and leverages it into a precise attack. We must understand the deep-rooted motivation of Satan to understand his schemes.

When challenged to answer the question, "Why does Satan do what he does?" the answer inevitably sounds something like, "To separate us from God." There may be an additional statement like, "So we go to hell." I hope this strikes a chord and reminds you of sin and death's motivation—"to separate us from God and his Church." It would even make sense for Satan to have the same motivation as sin and death because if we are honest to this point, many of us assume that Satan, sin, and death are interchangeable. "The devil made me do it." "Satan is working hard on _____ right now." The reality is that in any given situation, it could easily be sin, death, and/or Satan or some other demon. Here we cannot afford to be ignorant.

> *"All warfare is based on deception. Hence, when we are able to attack, we must seem unable; when using our forces, we must appear inactive; when we are near, we must make the enemy believe we are far away; when far away, we must make him believe we are near."*

—Sun Tzu, *The Art of War*

Satan is the father of lies (John 8:44). He wants to disguise his purposes to confuse us and make us vulnerable. Don't be confused. His desire is not to send us to hell, as if we are the pinnacle of creation. His desire is much loftier than the destruction of mortals. The prophet Isaiah illuminates the point in Satan's story when he falls into sin.

> *"How you are fallen from heaven, O Day Star, son of Dawn! How you are cut down to the ground, you who laid the nations low! You said in your heart, 'I will ascend to heaven; above the stars of God I will set my throne on high; I will sit on the mount of assembly in the far reaches of the north; I will ascend above the heights of the clouds; I will make myself like the Most High.' But you are brought down to Sheol, to the far reaches of the pit."*

—Isaiah 14:12–15

This is the moment when Lucifer's zeal for the glory of the LORD moved from cherishing to covetousness. Such a quick trick, a slight movement, sin makes. He takes the things we cherish most, some of our biggest blessings, and uses them against us. In sin, we want the gift more than the giver. Not only that, we want not just the gift, but all the giver has. Satan's downfall and his deep-rooted motivation is to attain the glory of God for himself.[7] To be as overt as possible: *Satan's desire, above all else, is to be God.* What does every number two want to be? Number one. What do you think pushed Laszlo Cseh and Chad Le Clos, Olympic swimmers widely considered ranked in the top three in the world, further than their capabilities and past their breaking point for each lap in the pool? The idea of standing on the podium atop Michael Phelps. While some refer to second place as first loser, I admit my athletic ability rarely allows me to even win at losing, so I would love to even get second place. But try and imagine the drive for those elite. Satan desires God's glory for himself.

The glory of God, as depicted in many End Times texts, reveals the glory of God as seen from the heavenly realms. It is absolutely astounding. Even with the most vigorous imagination, it is just out of comprehension. Psalm 113:4 keeps it simple: *"The LORD is high above all nations, and his glory above the heavens!"* Talk about fighting a losing battle. Satan's desire that he could somehow stage a coup that would result in him sitting on the throne of the Ancient of Days is laughable. God's glory is uncontainable by even the heavens...it's so marvelous it's terrifying. The earth is filled with the glory of God as well. For example, Habakkuk 2:14 states, *"For the earth will be filled with the knowledge of the glory of the LORD as the waters cover the sea."* And Numbers 14:21 says, *"But truly, as I live, and as all the earth shall be filled with the glory of the LORD."* These texts depict the revelation of the Son of God; this Gospel holds the purpose for all creation. Psalms 104:31 ties the creative work of God to his glory: *"May the glory of the LORD endure forever, may the LORD rejoice in his works."* From the Creation accounts in Genesis, we see that God delights in his handiwork. This is the expression of his will and the object of his affection. To boil it down: the creation's supreme work is to reflect the glory of God, for God has dominion over all things. This is where Satan makes his stand. Since God's glory is displayed in his dominion over all creation, Satan's ability to have influence over God's creation in a twisted way perverts God's glory for himself. He gets to pretend he is God by pushing us to submit to his will instead of God's.

As Jesus took on flesh and became man, Satan seized the opportunity to tempt Jesus in the wilderness. In this three-wave assault, Satan finishes by showing his hand—his true intention.

> *"Again, the devil took him to a very high mountain and showed him all the kingdoms of the world and their glory. And he said to him, 'All these I will give you, if you will fall down and worship me.' Then Jesus said to him, 'Be gone, Satan! For it is written, "You shall worship the LORD your God and him only shall you serve."'"*

—Matthew 4:8–10

What this means is that Satan's will is always the antithesis of God's will. It has to be. If it were in line with God's will, Satan would have to submit to the dominion of God, and at that point release desire for God's glory, which he cannot do. So, if God wants something, Satan will fill the space outside of God's will in an attempt to win God's glory for himself. In other words, if God's will is for us to love him before all else, Satan desires that we love anything and everything more than God. In this way he pretends that his dominion is before God's, and thus his glory.

By now you have probably begun to connect the dots between sin, death, and the devil. It's not that Satan, sin, and death are friends. It's more like the saying, "The enemy of my enemy is my friend" and more like the Axis powers of WWII. It's not that Germany and Japan were friends. They simply shared the same enemy, which made Japan a useful tool against America and the Allied powers. Sin is a useful tool in Satan's guerilla-war against God. It is much easier to influence creation when it is being isolated and separated from God and his Church. There is an easy opportunity here, and a sobering reality. If Satan's will is everything that is against God, then every time we sin, we not only reject God, but we also submit ourselves to the indirect will of Satan and glorify him in our actions.

> *"You are of your father the devil, and your will is to do your father's desires. He was a murderer from the beginning, and does not stand in the truth, because there is no truth in him. When he lies, he speaks out of his own character, for he is a liar and the father of lies."*

—John 8:44

> *"Whoever makes a practice of sinning is of the devil, for the devil has been sinning from the beginning. The reason the Son of God appeared was to destroy the works of the devil."*

—1 John 3:8

CHAPTER 8

When the Thief Comes

Conflict with demonic forces has been a regular part of my life and ministry. I have a few firsthand accounts of dealing with these spirits, but this book is not the place to detail those experiences. If you have such questions, feel free to reach out. The purpose of this chapter is to make you aware of some of the regular workings of evil spirits, including Satan. So, to help you focus on them in the chapters to come, I will ease some of your questions first.

HOW DO I KNOW IF I AM BEING ATTACKED BY EVIL SPIRITS?

I hunt rattlesnakes in the spring. There's an old saying, "For every snake you find, you have walked past five." In the same vein, when an evil spirit has been present on the attack, I've been confident I was able to recognize it. However, in reality, I'm sure I've missed many more than I have noticed. For the ones I did recognize, sometimes there were artifacts of spiritually evil practices (magic, voodoo, etc.). Sometimes there were anomalies that didn't make sense (temperatures, objects moving, animal behavior, etc.). Sometimes I could just feel the weight of it in the room. I realize this doesn't make it clear. Just realize that this is to the advantage of the enemy and probably part of his intent.

WHAT DO I DO IF I THINK I AM BEING ATTACKED OR A SPIRIT IS PRESENT?

Contact your pastor. If you don't have a pastor, ask a friend until you find someone you can trust. Tell them your story and invite them into your situation. Matthew 18:20 says, *"For where two or three are gathered in my name, there am I among them."*

HOW DO I FIGHT BACK AGAINST EVIL SPIRITS, OR GET RID OF THEM?

My last answer holds the key. First, reach out to your church. No man, in and of themselves, is capable of dominating Satan or any other demon. However, there is one man, the Son of God, in whose name the demons flee. *"The 72 returned with joy, saying, 'LORD, even the demons are subject to us in your name!'"* (Luke 10:17). But be careful of the demon's schemes, for even by the power of Jesus, we can be tempted to covet and desire the credit. Learning from Adam and Eve in the garden, we want to be in control. Never forget that it's Jesus, by the work of the Holy Spirit, that removes these thorns from us. Even Jesus warns, *"Nevertheless, do not rejoice in this, that the spirits are subject to you, but rejoice that your names are written in heaven"* (Luke 10:20). Rejoice in knowing that Jesus will never leave nor forsake you and will triumph on your behalf over all the spiritually evil forces.

"But he gives more grace. Therefore it says, "God opposes the proud but gives grace to the humble." Submit yourselves therefore to God. Resist the devil, and he will flee from you. Draw near to God, and he will draw near to you."

—James 4:6–8a

The process of casting out a demon varies from church to church. Generally, it starts with prayer, asking the LORD to intervene. It includes asking the LORD for blessing and holding fast to the promise of his blessing. Sometimes it requires fasting and prayer with the support of more members of the Body of Christ. I have a team of brothers, fellow laborers in the Gospel, whom I call on for support whenever I am faced with this responsibility. You too would be wise to seek out a few trusted friends who will pray and fast on your behalf, and you theirs.

HOW CAN I BE SURE IT'S A DEMON AND NOT SIN OR DEATH OR SOMETHING ELSE?

I start by taking an inventory of what's happening and how I'm feeling pressed. Often, when an evil spirit is present, they are bringing with them all kinds of temptation into sin. So, we have to deal with each one by the means God offers. To disarm the evil spirit, we remove the guilt and isolation of sin by confessing it and receiving forgiveness. (As I mentioned earlier, this is best done with another person—Matthew 18:20.) Then we deal with the spirit directly—running not to the crucifixion of Jesus on my behalf, but to his Lordship, the risen King, as he sits at the right hand of the Father at whom every knee will bow (Romans 14:11). Satan does not get to have dominion over that which Jesus the Christ, the Son of the Living God, has claimed as his own!

WHAT KINDS OF THINGS CAN I EXPECT SATAN TO DO TO ME?

"Float like a butterfly. Sting like a bee."—Muhammad Ali. Be quick on your feet, and don't be wherever you are expected to be. He is crafty and has ancient and vast wisdom of the human condition. In the rest of this chapter, we will look at some of the general ways this ancient enemy works.

THE MAN BEHIND THE CURTAIN

In the iconic movie, *The Wizard of Oz*, we follow the story of Dorothy and friends on their way to the Wizard of Oz. When they arrive at his home in the Emerald City, they are stricken with fear at the terrible sight of the *great and powerful* Oz, a huge green head with bursts of flame at every utterance—a sight that strikes fear even in the bravest of lions. But when Toto pulls back the curtain, Dorothy and the gang discover that behind the facade is a small, old man with bright cheeks and wispy blonde hair. He is very sweet on all accounts. The scarecrow calls the Wizard a "humbug," which he openly admits. Then Dorothy declares, "You're a very bad man," and the Wizard pleads, "Oh no my dear! I'm a very good man. I'm just a very bad wizard." Well, a humbug is a name for a deceiver, and the lie he told Dorothy was the biggest of them all.

Earlier in the movie, he had promised Dorothy a trip home, Scarecrow a brain, Tin Man a heart, and the Lion courage, only if they defeat the witch. When they return to collect the bounty, the green head casts them aside, saying come back tomorrow. He has no intention of fulfilling his promises. But now, upon the discovery of his secret, when questioned about the fulfillment of his promises to the Lion, the Tin Man, and the Scarecrow, he takes a completely different attitude than he did moments before. He willingly and enthusiastically points to the solution of their problems. He presents himself as their savior and teacher, but in reality, he tricks the heroes into believing that they are completely self-sufficient and that by offering fast words and trinkets, he no longer has to fulfill his promises, which you'll notice, he never does. After all, he is still the same humbug. How is it one minute he is a jerk, and the next he is a best friend? I think he is nothing more than a con man looking to manipulate people. It seems to me that one minute this man uses fear tactics, along with smoke and mirrors, to control people, and the next minute he uses fancy philosophies and toys to do the same thing. He truly is the most cunning villain of the story. Sorry if I just ruined the movie.

Satan is such a wizard. Satan will don whatever mask necessary to confuse and manipulate humanity, whether he presents himself as a fearsome foe, or as a benevolent BFF. What we must remember is that no matter which face Satan is wearing, he is still a humbug—a deceiver. So be on high alert because it is so easy to get caught up in his schemes and forget the truth.

THE GIANT GREEN HEAD

It's easy for those of you reading this book to be wary of the fearsome foe that is the devil. Within Christianity, we are always quick to point to the movements and actions of Satan when he behaves in this manner. We cry wolf, and true to the saying, we find that many times when we cry out, there's no wolf actually present. I remember all the Christian fear surrounding *Harry Potter* as satanic or demonic. I've read the series and I can tell you, there is no wolf. But I guess that's the trick. While we're busy crying wolf, we forget to watch for the lion.

"Be sober-minded; be watchful. Your adversary the devil

prowls around like a roaring lion, seeking someone to devour."

—I Peter 5:8

Yes, a lion is a predator with very similar hunting strategies to a wolf, but the lion still functions differently. To write this book, I went on a safari in Kenya to see the lions firsthand. I wish! No, I didn't, but I did watch some YouTube videos. When I lived in southern Georgia, I took a young airman predator hunting at a local farm. We got to the farm after dusk (it's legal to hunt predators at night). Ahead of us about 60 yards, just in the trees, we heard what sounded like the scream of a woman being brutally attacked, and yet not really human. A little unhinged, we followed the road into the trees and around to the first field. We climbed the 20- foot-tall hunting blind and took a deep breath of relief. The first scream was now at our 3 o'clock, and over the next hour we heard the scream two more times, once at our 12 o'clock and the third at our 10 o'clock—each over 200 yards away in the trees across the field. Then all at once we heard the scream again...about 50 yards away...at our 6 o'clock. We turned to look out the back of the blind and saw nothing but darkness in the forest that butted up to our backs.

I asked the owner of the property what he thought that might have been. In wonderful good-ole-boy style, he offered his own description of the sound, which I can't repeat, and then said, "That's the Florida panther." Later that year we caught a glimpse of its tail on a trail camera. If you want to get a sense of the "mountain lion scream", search it on YouTube. It is an unsettling feeling to know you are not the apex predator in the woods. It's even worse when you realize you're being investigated by one. Worst of all is when you're being stalked by one. The lion wants you to think it's over there, and then over here, when all the while it's searching for your weakest point, which is where he will strike.

Fear can be a very valuable motivator. In fact, the Bible is littered with urgings to fear, but they all center on God. Fear him, for he is unlimited and infinitely uncontrollable. The Hebrew word for "fear," when used in our relationship with God, brings to mind reverence and awe, which are key components in worship. Considering God's capabilities and capacity helps teach us John the Baptist's final lesson and the heart of our worship: *"He must increase, I must decrease"* (John 3:30).

People will suggest I have a fear of heights, but I don't. I have a fear of falling, and that fear has led me to many decisions that have ensured my survival and safety. While fears can be useful tools for a healthy life, they can also be exploited in severely detrimental ways. Fear is regularly used in power plays. Fear has been the tool used throughout history to dominate others, from person over person, to nation over nation. Fear moves us past rationality and logic to respond with base human urges. Then our survival instincts kick in with fight-or-flight reactions. Satan uses all kinds of tactics to produce and exploit fear in order to dominate us.

Let's look at Jesus' second temptation from Satan, where Satan takes Jesus to the pinnacle of the Temple and suggests he jump. The principle is that if Satan can entice Jesus to sin, he indirectly submits to the will of Satan, and Satan finally has what he always wanted—authority over God. The stakes are high, and Satan exploits the fear of falling by using scripture to try and trick Jesus into sin, saying, "God won't let you pancake on the street" (Matthew 4:5–6). Fear changes how we think. Consider this: although we know God is in control and has given each of us blessings, fear moves us to worry, which is debilitating. It enslaves our joy and even our relationships. It changes how we treat others and ourselves. If you've had a teen or been a teen, you're probably familiar with the "suffocating" phenomenon teens experience. When parents do that helicopter thing, which ultimately deteriorates the relationship between the worried parent and now rebellious teen, the teen turns to lying and isolation from their parents. At the moment we give in to that fear, we submit to Satan's will.

Have you ever watched lions? Not the ones in the zoo, but the ones in the wild. They are still very lethargic creatures, making slow, relatively small movements. Even on the hunt they hide their full force and capability in order to use the least amount of energy to accomplish their goals. Most often, Satan will use our fears against us in order to utilize what is already present, to cause mass effect with minimal effort. He enjoys cultural phenomena that move unknowing people to fear him indirectly. He also takes the direct approach by *causing* us to fear him. Like the lion stalking in the woods, he inspires fear so that we flee at the sound of "he who must not be named." Think of all the benefits he has reaped from movies like *The Exorcist* or *The Nun*: the unknown power and force of darkness. Fear causes flight to kick in and we abandon everything. Like the friends who met the bear in the woods, "I only have to outrun you..." This has been the regular tactic in communities where spiritualism is foundational. He will use smoke and mirrors to try and dominate the community through witch doctors and shamans, a terrific display of power that forces the people into silent submission.

Peter depicts Satan deliberately as a lion, as its presence necessitates an amount of caution. Peter says, "Be sober-minded; be watchful." What this means is be cautious of what you are exposing yourself to. Consider what you are letting inside. We have so many wonderful senses, yet it's through them that the devil and demonic forces have access to influence us and ultimately enslave us. It's crazy to me that people can willingly open themselves up to this kind of influence with Ouija boards, fortune tellers and tarot cards, like a hiker with a 20-ounce steak hanging out of the back of his jeans. "In case you're looking for an opportunity, lion, my backside is exposed." Before you watch that movie, play that game, read that fortune, ask yourself: who has authority in this situation, and what am I opening myself up to? When you read those stories or visit that online community, are you pitching your tent at the outskirts of camp? Are you opening yourself up? Satan and the demonic forces are always looking for your weakest point—the chink in the armor—to exploit your weakness for mass damage. So, we must be on guard!

If you are living with debilitating fear, how then do you proceed? Take the advice of Jesus in the Sermon on the Mount: *"But seek first the kingdom of God and his righteousness, and all these things will be added to you as well."* First pray, asking the Lord to bless this exercise as you search for his will and his ways. Start with where you are now, in this moment, and process how you have come to this point, considering all the blessings of your life and your greatest treasures. Who has maintained and provided for all your needs and given you these cherished and common things, like home, food, work, and the extraordinary things? Who has caused the barren couple to have a child? Then move to the challenges you have faced and who has delivered you. Who has opened a door when all others closed? Who has said to your cancers, "Here and no further—now you will depart!"? Is it not the Lord? Now let your gaze rise toward the infinite capability and majesty of his expressed and unfathomable will. His righteousness, like the train of his surcoat, fills the temple (Isaiah. 6:1). He. Can. Do. Anything. He too has been depicted as a Lion (Revelation 5:5)—not as a hidden predator, but as the King of the Pride. In a millisecond, sinews snap, muscles contract, and with 1,000 psi, jaws close with brute force at his whim and will. A Mufasa to Satan's Scar...if Scar were a red-headed step-child of no relation (no offense to the Weasleys out there). Tell me: which is worthy of fear? Rest assured, he is not a tame lion, but he is good. [8] It's his faithful goodness that fulfills his promise, *"You will keep in perfect peace him whose mind is steadfast, because he trusts in You"* (Isaiah 26:3). Finally, set aside time to search the scriptures each time fear tries to assail you, and see what promises God has given you where he promises his faithfulness. Let his faithfulness fill the void that fear is leaving in your life.

THE CARNIE

The giant green-headed wizard of Oz is very easy to spot. Fear is always brought to center stage, which means when it steps forward, it's hard to miss and simultaneously presents the circumstance to deal with it. Though it is an uncomfortable process, it's hard to overlook. For the Christian, that means fear is easier to deal with than the other much more common face of the wizard, the man behind the curtain: the carnie. There is no question that the green head is great and terrible in his presentation, but it's the carnie who is tricky. Like any carnival worker, with a smile and a wave he invites you to a simple and entertaining game that requires minimal skill to win your prize. For only a dollar and a couple of rings on a few milk jars, you win a huge unicorn. Twenty dollars and an "I'm a sucker" key chain later, you realize you've been had.

Earlier in Part One, I mentioned the conversation I had with my great-grandmother when I knew I was going to become a pastor. She was already 101 years old and enduring dementia, and the first time I told her, with love in her eyes she asked, "And you're going dancing?" (I was headed out to go line dancing that evening). Then she leaned over with a mischievous grin and whispered, "You're not going to be a very good pastor." She was old school! As I said, I told her another time after that and when she began to tear up, I was terrified my footloose Fridays were leading her to tears. But she said those words that have stuck with me: "The devil is going to attack you so much more now." Her long faith life and wisdom saw the reality. Satan has much more to gain in dominating people already in the Church than others, so we must be on guard all the more because his focus is on the Church.

I find that Satan presents himself to the Church like the carnie much more often than the fearmonger. It's not a face of fear; it's with a face of friendship where he alters reality so slightly that it's almost unnoticeable. Let's look again at Jesus' temptation in the wilderness. In

Matthew 4:6, Satan quotes Psalm 91:11–12, changing the context to try to cause Jesus to slip into sin. He uses the words of scripture to try and hide the game. The ease of altering the meaning of the text, combined with inattentive, unknowing Christians, empowers Satan to lead us into all kinds of sin. He invites us to "step right up" and paints a worldview that is very attractive. *"But the serpent said to the woman, 'You will not surely die...your eyes will be opened, and you will be like God, knowing good and evil.' So when the woman saw that the tree was good for food, and that it was a delight to the eyes..."* (Genesis 3:4–6a). We think we are guaranteed success, but the truth is, we've lost the farm in the process. Throughout the history of the Church, there have been many heretics who have offered skewed interpretation of the scriptures. Though enemies to the Truth, none had malicious intent. In fact, I would be surprised to find a heretic who wasn't zealous for their beliefs and desired to help the Church, not hinder it. It's this ignorance that is so dangerous. It looks good, it feels good, it feels right, and yet it's a rigged game that results in losers, not winners. Did you remember the tagline from that magician movie *Now You See Me*? "Come in close, because the more you think you see, the easier it'll be to fool you." Satan will always try to pervert the power of the Truth, our LORD Jesus Christ, and the Word to win dominance for himself.

CHAPTER 9

Constant Vigilance!

"Therefore, my beloved, as you have always obeyed, so now, not only as in my presence but much more in my absence, work out your own salvation with fear and trembling, for it is God who works in you, both to will and to work for his good pleasure."

—Philippians 2:12–13

"Slothfulness casts into a deep sleep, and an idle person will suffer hunger."

—Proverbs 19:15

"Constant Vigilance!" Mad-eye Moody's mantra echoes in my mind. Idleness is our enemy. As Solomon points out, laziness leads to lack. If we don't tend the field, sow the seeds, and water them when it's time for harvest, we have empty stomachs. This is also true spiritually. If we allow ourselves to be idle in our faith, to sleep in a stupor when Satan comes to call, he finds a hungry belly. *An empty stomach is a powerful motivator that creates covetousness, which leads to gluttony.* Jesus taught it this way.

> *"When the unclean spirit has gone out of a person, it passes through waterless places seeking rest, but finds none. Then it says, 'I will return to my house from which I came.' And when it comes, it finds the house empty, swept, and put in order. Then it goes and brings with it seven other spirits more evil than itself, and they enter and dwell there, and the last state of that person is worse than the first."*

—Matthew 12:43–45a

What are we being filled with? Of course there are many dangers in this world. I have described some to this point, but there are also dangers within the Church. There is no question that Christian doctrine in America is eroding and being replaced with politics. The Kingdom of Heaven is being traded for self-satisfying worldviews. On another front, we find the desire for prosperity (fueled by capitalism and the "American dream") has created a mass movement in Christendom called the "prosperity gospel." Chances are you are familiar with prosperity gospel preachers; you might even find one of their books in your home. This is a dominant focus of the Church in the United States. Go to your local Christian bookstore. You'll see mountains and mountains of self-help books, but very few classics of theology, even for pastors! We skip on the nurturing of faith through the pursuit of God and look for quick ways to get what others have: happiness, joy, security, healthy marriages, well-rounded children, and ministries of effectiveness and influence. Covetousness is a dangerous sin and the mother of lust (not just sexual) that strips us down to a single focus and mind. It becomes the jewel of our kingdom as we sit on the throne of our hearts. This is what the would-be king needs to be happy. "We swears to serve the master of the precious. We will swear on the...on the precious." - Sméagol, *Lord of the Rings*. (Did you read that in the Sméagol voice? I hope so.) The only way to manage these dangers is to maintain a healthy spiritual diet. Fill up on the Truth and the hope of his promises. Let these words of Jesus dwell on you. Read them a few times; let them sink in.

> *"And he opened his mouth and taught them, saying:*
>
> *'Blessed are the poor in spirit, for theirs is the kingdom of heaven.*
>
> *Blessed are those who mourn, for they shall be comforted.*
>
> *Blessed are the meek, for they shall inherit the earth.*
>
> *Blessed are those who hunger and thirst for righteousness, for they shall be satisfied.*
>
> *Blessed are the merciful, for they shall receive mercy.*
>
> *Blessed are the pure in heart, for they shall see God.*
>
> *Blessed are the peacemakers, for they shall be called sons of God.*
>
> *Blessed are those who are persecuted for righteousness' sake, for theirs is the kingdom of heaven.*
>
> *Blessed are you when others revile you and persecute you and utter all kinds of evil against you falsely on my account. Rejoice and be glad, for your reward is great in heaven, for so they persecuted the prophets who were before you.'"*

—Matthew 5:2–12

Have you ever tried to change your eating habits? You schedule, you prepare, and plan. Something happens and you are hungry, really hungry. Where do you go? I go to Chick-fil-A, which isn't great because I have a gluten and dairy intolerance. Did I mention I always order an Oreo shake? Man, those taste good! Covetousness to fill my empty stomach also breeds gluttony—"Uh, yeah, I want a large." I don't feel good after I eat it, and it doesn't fill the need but rather, makes it worse. Einstein says the definition of insanity is doing the same thing over and over again and expecting a different result. Well, I guess I'm nuts, because in my gluttony I keep overeating what's not healthy, expecting it to fill me up and it never does. Around and around the circle we go. Gluttony isn't just for eating or drinking. The need to be valued is pervasive. With the deconstruction of community, we see it first in the kids, as they invest countless hours in social media to try and find some kind of validation.

To feel value, we offer our character as collateral, pushing others down to make ourselves feel good. We offer our values, willing to take the shortcut and sacrifice what's important to get ahead. We sacrifice our bodies to try and move others to love us. When we feel a hole in our lives, a vacancy, we tend to respond by overcompensating. There have been countless violent acts in our society, from children to seniors, in recent decades, notwithstanding the silent killers like depression and abuse. All of these find a motivation in gluttony, overcompensating to meet a need. What if I told you it's perfectly okay to have low self-esteem, to feel the need to be valued, to be validated, to be seen? Jesus promises that he has come to bind up the brokenhearted and to show you unconditional love. Jesus has come to be your king, to rule over your life, and to be sovereign over all of your hardships, struggles, joys, and delights. He has come that you may have life to the full. The Truth says, "I have come to be the king of your heart." Satan says, "Be the king of your own heart (subtext: and I'll be the king of you)." Read again the promises of Matthew 5:2–10 that Jesus makes to you. Pray with David,

"The LORD is my shepherd; I shall not want," even in the deepest darkest cell, lost in our battle with sin. Jesus is with you, knows what you're going through, and is coming soon to put all these enemies under his feet.

FILLING UP IN FAITH

"Not that I am speaking of being in need, for I have learned in whatever situation I am to be content. I know how to be brought low, and I know how to abound. In any and every circumstance, I have learned the secret of facing plenty and hunger, abundance and need. I can do all things through him who strengthens me."

—Philippians 4:12–14

Max Lucado wrote a wonderful children's book titled, *"You Are Special."* It teaches the importance of spending time with God to help combat the evil forces of the world. God invites us to come sit with him, every day, and he will live this life with us. The words of Paul to the church in Philippi speak to Paul's constant time with God and encourage the congregation in that pursuit. Paul is an amazing example of faithful stewardship. He is responsible for writing most of the New Testament and for building churches throughout the Mediterranean. His faith kept him through suffering and celebration, life and even martyrdom in Rome, but there is one important truth to learn from his life. He never did it alone. The Holy Spirit was, of course, with him and led the ministry through him, but the Holy Spirit also equipped him with support—brothers and sisters in the faith who supported him, prayed for him, and labored with him. This is the beautiful blessing Jesus gives each of us. He gives us one another, as the community, the Body of Christ in the Holy Spirit to support, love, nurture, and labor together.

There are all kinds of spiritual disciplines you can add to your life to fill you up and be present in your relationship with God. In our church we have eight life tools we use to disciple followers and help them grow in their spiritual lives. I myself have spent years discipling people and teaching them how to disciple others. One thing I've learned is that no one is good at all of them. In fact, I myself am good at teaching and vision casting, but it is very challenging for me to offer sympathy and empathy. I really have to work at it. It's not that I don't desire to do those things. It's just that they don't come naturally. For me, this is the blessing of the church. Not that I can just let someone else handle this stuff so I don't have to engage in sharing burdens, but people who have been wired naturally through the Holy Spirit to be sympathetic and empathetic can lead and teach me.

I went to Alcoholics Anonymous meetings that were held at my church in southern Georgia. This group was a regular place for folks who were in rehab or new to the program to get support. One of the "old timers" often spoke at the meetings. He would talk for a long time, sometimes running down all kinds of bunny trails. I would find myself wondering if this is how people on Sundays feel. But at some point, every Thursday, he would say, "For you newcomers, look around. If you want to be a winner, sit with winners; if you want to be a loser, sit with losers." In other words, look for people who have had a similar experience and some success in their journey. Invest yourself in their life and see what you can learn. Therefore, it is more important for you to find a community of faith that has some success in the journey, rather than to be a master of your Christian disciplines. But be careful how you measure success. If you invest your life in a faith community that looks like a carnival, then expect carnies to take advantage of you.

TAKEAWAYS

DEVIL'S GOAL: Lucifer wants to be God, to have God's glory.

DEVIL'S TACTICS: Your purpose in life is to reflect the glory of God, as he has dominion over all things. Satan tries to steal God's glory by getting you to submit to his will, using sin and death as pawns.

GOD'S VICTORY: No man, in and of themselves, is capable of dominating Satan or any other demon. However, there is one man, the Son of God, in whose name the demons flee. That name... Jesus.

ACTION POINT: Commit yourself, your suffering, and your weakness to the LORD. Keep your focus on the grace of God, as Jesus has made you his own. He will never leave you nor forsake you. Trust in his faithfulness and sovereignty.

Part Two

Christian Living, with a Mission

A WORD FROM
SAMWISE GAMGEE

"It's like in the great stories Mr. Frodo. The ones that really mattered. Full of darkness and danger they were, and sometimes you didn't want to know the end. Because how could the end be happy? How could the world go back to the way it was when so much bad happened? But in the end, it's only a passing thing, this shadow. Even darkness must pass. A new day will come. And when the sun shines it will shine out the clearer."

—Lord of the Rings: The Two Towers

IT'S IN THE MIDDLE OF a battle that hope seems most elusive. It may seem that I have painted a discouraging picture of the spiritual life up to this point. I might have simply described the water you're drowning in, namely, the challenges you currently face. I have brought into contrast the spiritual enemies that you wrestle with throughout your mortal life—the tricks, lies, and challenges they bring that often overcome us throughout our journey. Yet, there is hope. As Paul says,

"We are afflicted in every way, but not crushed; perplexed, but not driven to despair; persecuted, but not forsaken; struck down, but not destroyed; always carrying in the body the death of Jesus, so that the life of Jesus may also be manifested in our bodies. For we who live are always being given over to death for Jesus' sake, so that the life of Jesus also may be manifested in our mortal flesh."

—2 Corinthians 4:8–11

By our LORD Jesus, God has provided the completion of the two greatest gifts he has given us, the Law and the Gospel. These tools are prepared for your right and left hands (2 Corinthians 6:7b) that you may grasp the Sword of the Spirit (Ephesians 6:17b) and apply it to those spiritual enemies and all their wicked schemes in order to guard your heart in faith and all those around you. Take hold of these next chapters like ancient Jedi texts, and learn not only to handle the Word of God, but *to breathe...just breathe... reach out with your feelings* and listen for what the Holy Spirit is doing in every circumstance. (I hope you read that with Mark Hamill's voice.)

Law and Gospel: these may be familiar words, but more than likely, they have a different reference in your mind than the one I am presenting. So, allow me to bring clarity to these two foundations of the scriptures. I am not speaking to books of the Bible directly—not Matthew's, Mark's, Luke's, John's, or Moses'. They are not confined to one to the Old and the other to the New Testaments. In fact, you will find the most emphatic display of the Law in the New Testament and some of the most expansive descriptions of the Gospel in the Old. The Law is not man-made, nor is the Gospel. The Law of God and the Gospel of God share in origin and purpose. They both are from God and are for the purpose of salvation. The Gospel is not merely spiritual, nor is the Law. They are beneficial tools given for the daily lives and relationships of all people. Put simply, Doctor of Theology Martin Luther writes, "The law says, 'Do this,' and it is never done. Grace says, 'Believe in this, and everything is already done.'"[9]

Living in the post-1950s Christian worldview, even people without personal experience in Christian community still have experience with what is considered the "Law of God" or Christian rules. Sadly, very few have experience with the Gospel. Many of those laws resonate in the hearts of the people expected to conform to them. These people are within and outside the church—it makes no difference. However, when that is the only vantage point from which one is seeing God, the result is always the rejection of a mean god. So before we can delve further into these gifts, I want to point back to an earlier statement I will use as the foundation of our learning. We must hold onto it as the bedrock of our existence. Both the Law and the Gospel have the same origin. That origin is the Force. Just kidding.

CHAPTER 10

God's Love

The Law and the Gospel originate with God. Both are full of his justice, mercy, grace, and most importantly, his love. It's God's love that moves him to reach out to his creation and draw us to himself. It's his love that shapes how we see ourselves. If children lose sight of their parent's love for them, any law they give is hollow and pointless. So is any grace. The relationship is broken, like a heart on AFib. I want to share with you my absolute favorite verse that I shared with my daughter at her baptism, and my hope is that it may wash over your heart as well.

> "The LORD your God is with you. A mighty one who will save; He will rejoice over you with gladness; he will quiet you with his love; He will rejoice over you with singing."
>
> —Zephaniah 3:17

I love this verse. Regardless of the dark cell I'm locked in, the summit I have risen to, or the valley that lies ahead, the LORD my God is with me. Just as he promised in Isaiah 57:15... he is in a high and lofty place but also with me in my low times and sorrow. Know that the LORD (who through generations of faithfulness has become so familiar to even the youngest of his people) is with you and is the source of comfort. No matter how far sin and death might try to separate you, God is with you and he is mighty for your salvation. He is like a lion who appears to spend most of his life lethargic but at the right moment, a trigger, snaps into fierce action, and the strength of his loins is almost frightening at the speed of its engagement as he snaps into action. The LORD is ready to display the wonder of his strength in pursuit of your rescue. He will never hold back as he continually seeks your safety. He is always winning for you with so much fierce power and purpose. It's humbling to sit and consider.

However, the rest of the verse is what is so enthralling. "He will rejoice over you with gladness." When the Father sees his son from far off and runs to him, he doesn't hide his face or chastise the boy. He embraces him with smiles full of teeth and restores the boy, calling to the servants to exclaim the joy of having his son back.

In our house, we just finished potty training. It's a weird thing to rejoice with a child because they pooped, especially when you hear the screams all over the house, "Come wipe my butt!" Yet with new joy at each moment of his life, we rejoice at his experience, as smelly and gross as it may be, because he is our son and we love him. If your parents looked for every opportunity to point out your failures, it might be tough to look past that in order to see a loving father who looks at you with joy. But that is exactly how your Father in Heaven looks on you and your experience, no matter the crap involved.

The prophet then says, "He will quiet you with his love." It was 2001, and Allan Chapman, a long-time choir director, was coaching our show choir. He was trying to help us portray to the audience the love being communicated in our ballad. Okay, focus. Yes, I was in show choir all through high school, and yes, that amounted to a lot of singing and dancing in lots of sequins, and no, I am not going to tell you our group name so you can search YouTube. Back to the story. Allan got very quiet, commanding the attention of 50 teens with a whisper. I remember it as if it were yesterday. He whispered, "Some of the most important things you will ever hear or say in your life will be uttered at little more than a whisper, when words fail to capture the depth of what is happening." *I love you. We're having a baby. I'm dying.* The truth is that some things are so deep, so wide that our frail language can't bear the weight of them and we are just left in awe. Zephaniah says to watch for the sheer love of God that would be coming into the world in his one and only Son to heal our infirmities and promise hope for the future. And that God was willing to subject himself to torture and murder. His unyielding willingness to offer himself for you and for me cost him his life. At the sight of it, words fail. There is nothing you could utter to respond to the love he has for you each day of your life.

That is awe-inspiring love. The verse says, "He will rejoice over you with singing." Do you see that from the death and resurrection of Jesus on your behalf, God has redeemed and restored you? The very God who opened his mouth to speak creation into existence, "Let there be light," now opens his mouth to sing because of his love for you. I pray that the Father would open your heart and mind to the fullness of his love in the Law and the Gospel. *"So that Christ may dwell in your hearts through faith—that you, being rooted and grounded in love, may have strength to comprehend with all the saints what is the breadth and length and height and depth, and to know the love of Christ that surpasses knowledge, that you may be filled with all the fullness of God"* (Ephesians 3:17–19).

The love of God must be our most eager pursuit, not that we earn it, but that we may fully know it, live in the liberty of it, and have our worldview be changed by it. Consider the words of Paul:

"If I speak in the tongues of men and of angels, but have not love, I am a noisy gong or a clanging cymbal. And if I have prophetic powers, and understand all mysteries and all knowledge, and if I have all faith, so as to remove mountains, but have not love, I am nothing. If I give away all I have, and if I deliver up my body to be burned, but have not love, I gain nothing."

—1 Corinthians 13:1–3

If you lose sight of the love of God, your grasp of the Law and Gospel or any of the tools and gifts of God (even your mastery of eloquence and explanation of the articles of faith) are all just noise. No melody to the movement, no poetic verse to enlighten, just noise, like sixth-grade band concerts. Even the most learned of theologians who through reason search the Scriptures, without love, still know nothing. Faith loses meaning without God's love. If a faith community loses sight of the love of God, it will always follow these truths Paul sets in 1 Corinthians 13. It will sacrifice the will of God in the Law and the Gospel and pervert the message and purpose of the community.

First Corinthians 13, verses 4–7 are a wonderful, pragmatic way to train yourself to hold fast to God's love and to seek it out through your experience. Where you find the fruits of love you will find the work of the Holy Spirit, always witnessing to God's love.

"Love is patient and kind; love does not envy or boast; it is not arrogant or rude. It does not insist on its own way; it is not irritable or resentful; it does not rejoice at wrongdoing, but rejoices with the truth. Love bears all things, believes all things, hopes all things, endures all things."

—1 Corinthians 13:4–7

CHAPTER 11

The Law of God

The Law and the Gospel are fundamentally different, even though both flow from the will of God and are motivated by love for his creation in the hope of salvation. The Law and Gospel were given at different times with different components and purposes. The Law of God cannot be limited to the legal points given in the laws of Moses or any other place within the Old Testament. However, the legal demands of the Law do reflect the lower purpose of the Law of God, namely to maintain holiness and righteousness. The Law reveals the justice of God in his wrath against the ungodliness and unrighteousness of humanity as we suppress the truth (Romans 1:18). But do not assume this is a terrible thing. In our sin, we respond to the Law by rejecting its conviction because it is difficult to bear, not because the Law is bad. In fact, the Law has been revealing the spiritual attributes of God's power and nature since Genesis 1.[10] His justice and his mercy are always preparing for the revelation of his grace in Christ Jesus.

The Law was given to Moses as he recorded the generations of God's faithfulness from Adam to the Wandering. We see within those first five books of the Old Testament how God's Law was present and working in the lives of the patriarchs Adam, Noah, Abraham, Isaac, and Jacob to name a few, and all of this occurred long before Charlton Heston came down Mount Sinai with the Ten Commandments. God's will has been written on the hearts of men since the beginning of creation. His will is a reflection of his righteousness and holiness. Our consciences bear testament to the validity of the Law in our lives, deep within our inmost being. After Moses, the Law was still being displayed through the generations of God's people as they grappled with the standard of holiness and righteousness against their own sin.

> *"'Now therefore, if you will indeed obey my voice and keep my covenant, you shall be my treasured possession among all peoples, for all the earth is mine; and you shall be to me a kingdom of priests and a holy nation.' These are the words that you shall speak to the people of Israel."*

—Exodus 19:5

This has been the promise of the Law since the Creation: that by adherence, not just hearing but doing,[11] we will be holy and righteous. However, because of the Fall into sin we need salvation, and the Law is not capable of salvation. Sin seized the opportunity in the Garden to bring humanity into slavery under it. The Law set the bar when it described the standard of holiness and righteousness. This resulted in sin using the space under the bar to increase the trespass and reign in our bodies. The Law that promised life only brought death because of our sin.[12] This is not a bad thing because the Law then reveals sin to be sin and illuminates the distinction between the darkness and the light. The Law of God reveals sin by how sin responds to the Law.

THE MARKS OF THE LAW

Before we are presented with the Law, we are still enslaved by sin. Whether we are aware of it or not, sin binds us and leaves us for dead in a dark and lonely cell. In that darkness, we sit unaware of its hold on us and unaware of any hope of freedom. But in love, when the Holy Spirit shines the light of the Law into our darkness, we begin to see three things clearly.

Have you ever been in complete darkness? Your eyes have adjusted so you could almost make out shapes and varying degrees of black. Then when a light shines on you, without thinking, your natural reaction is to close your eyes and turn your face from the light. Its brightness is too drastic a contrast from your experience in the dark, and your eyes cannot immediately adjust to the change. In the same way, when the Law illuminates our experience, most often, depending on how much time we've had to adjust to the darkness, our first response is rejection. We are resilient creatures who are capable of all kinds of adaptations to survive. We can live in slavery for years and years, able to overlook shackles and isolation in order to establish comfort in normalcy. So, when the Law comes in to show us that we are living a life without liberty, we often lash out, trying to snuff out the light or hide from it because it's challenging our comfort. We've grown comfortable in the dark. When the Law exposes sin in our lives, we must, through our discomfort, not hide, but slowly, over many attempts if necessary, open our eyes and see what the Law has exposed. With courage, we must take an inventory of our circumstance so that we can move on.

As we take inventory of our sin, in addition to the circumstance it brought us to (the costs to our lives, relationships, hopes, and dreams), we must realize the Law is shining a light on the situation but is unable to change it, like a friend suggesting, "Hey, the solution to your problem is to stop sinning." It hits your ears like a lifeguard who sees you drowning and yells, "You should swim!" but you're still drowning. If I could swim, I wouldn't be in this situation! Hopelessness leads us to despair.

While this seems terrible, it's not because this severe discomfort is a powerful motivator. It pushes and prods us to exhaustive reflection, just as drowning draws you to reflect on the most basic of life's necessities. When you're drowning, you realize how precious oxygen is and how you've overlooked that precious gift. You realize how out-of-control we really are, even in familiar situations, and you're pushed to grapple with the reality of your circumstance and to cherish every small gift. It's the same thing with every near-death experience; it moves us to analyze our beliefs, values, and actions.

From despair, we consider all of the things that have been seized by sin and the damage that has occurred because of our submission to it. We realize how our willingness and negligence have played a part in bringing us to this point. Then the Law shines a peace in our hearts we had not realized—that we are wrong and sorry. It is an odd miracle that gifts us with serenity. It's a little warmth in a cold realization. We accept fault because it's at the point of realization and despair. Acceptance of failure pushes us to accept the justice of the circumstance and the need to be rescued from it. At this point, the Gospel must be proclaimed, for the Law is incapable of any hope. Without hope, despair will destroy us.

CHAPTER 12

The Gospel of God

MISCONCEPTIONS OF THE GOSPEL

1. The Gospel is—the books of the Bible

The Gospel is not merely the written accounts of the life and ministry of Jesus contained in the four gospels. Matthew, Mark, Luke, and John are all called gospels because of their subject matter. They contain the Gospel, the good news in the life and ministry of Jesus of Nazareth, the Christ, the Son of the Living God. The Gospel of God is found in almost every book of the Bible. In the words of the prophet Jeremiah: *"Thus says the LORD: 'The people who survived the sword found grace in the wilderness; when Israel sought for rest, the LORD appeared to him from far away. I have loved you with an everlasting love; therefore I have continued my faithfulness to you'"* (Jeremiah 31:2–3). And the prophet Isaiah, *"Comfort, comfort my people, says your God. Speak tenderly to Jerusalem, and cry to her that her warfare is ended, that her iniquity is pardoned, that she has received from the LORD's hand double for all her sins"* (Isaiah 40:1–2).

2. The Gospel is—all about humanity's salvation

Sin wants us to focus on ourselves because it's the quickest way to separate us from God. Sin seeps into our common misconception of the Gospel. We think the Good News of Jesus Christ is just the redemption of sinners. This could not be more wrong or deadly. As we focus on ourselves, we have a very high view of our place in creation. How many days of creation were there? Seven? Six? Only one really matters—the day they made humanity. I realize that doesn't make sense, but the way we interpret the Gospel leads us to believe that only humanity matters, that Jesus came to save *us* from our sins. It has led to the development of all kinds of theology, including the teaching that God will be destroying the earth and making a brand new one complete with its own Heaven. I have heard clergy fighting over whether all dogs go to Heaven. At these words I hear the dry voice of Luke Skywalker in *The Last Jedi*: "Amazing, every word of what you just said is wrong."

> *"For I consider that the sufferings of this present time are not worth comparing with the glory that is to be revealed to us. For the creation waits with eager longing for the revealing of the sons of God. For the creation was subjected to futility, not willingly, but because of him who subjected it, in hope that the creation itself will be set free from its bondage to corruption and obtain the freedom of the glory of the children of God. For we know that the whole creation has been groaning together in the pains of childbirth until now."*

—Romans 8:18–22

Paul says creation is waiting for the revelation of the sons of God, for it too was subjected to futility.[13] Why did creation reflect the sin of Adam? Because it too was meant to wait in *hope* that it will be freed through humanity from corruption. How is creation freed through humanity? The new Adam.[14] In the Creation accounts of Genesis chapter 1 and 2, God said each day that his creation was good and the completion of it, in its entirety, was "very good" (Genesis 1:31). So how could we possibly think that this story, God's redemptive plan, wasn't tailored with all creation in mind? The Greek word is translated as "new" in Revelation 21. A more literal translation *"renewed"* indicates the same resurrection sense of our LORD in which we have come to hope.[15] The hope of the Gospel reaches every aspect of our reality. It changes how we treat our bodies in the hope of the resurrection. It changes how we treat each other in the love of Jesus. It changes how we treat this world because it too has hope in Jesus.

THE GOSPEL IS AN ABIDING RELATIONSHIP

As I sit in this coffee shop, I look across the room and see a father sitting at a table across from his young daughter of probably four or five years old. He is just a regular guy, wearing jeans and a red t-shirt. He has a beard, tattoos on his forearms, and glasses. I can't stop looking at them (this is awkward) as he leans on the table and eagerly, with a face full of admiration, watches his little blonde eat a chocolate donut with pink sprinkles. She just nibbles away and his eyes twinkle, fixed on her. He is visibly delighted in this moment with her. He smiles and wipes her mouth, jokes with her, and laughs. They play little games while she savors this special treat. He gets extra napkins, wipes her hands, and cleans the table of the mess, all the while finding such joy in this special time he shares with his little girl. She hops out of her seat and bounds towards the door. The donut is gone so it's time to get on with her day. I didn't hear any "thank you" or "you're the best daddy," but I can tell from Dad's face that it wasn't necessary because the chance to do something special and be with his little girl was all he wanted.

This is the Gospel. Whether they stopped for a donut today or went straight to school, she knows he is her father. Whether she is listening to Dad or having a tough day, she never wonders who he is to her, nor does he. Some days, they might spend every waking moment together, whereas other days he might not even see her until he kisses her head late at night while she is fast asleep.

In the early years of their relationship he spends all his time hovering, watching and protecting, providing for her needs. The reward is a little girl who cries out "Daddy" when he gets home and races to give him a hug and a smoochy. In the teen years he will spend less time with her and more time on the sidelines watching and sharing in her triumphs and failures. He will hear more, "Get out of my room" and, "Don't look at my phone." But he is watching the time, ready to pick her up and drive her home, to hold her through every tear, every broken heart, and tell her it's going to be okay. He will watch her grow and walk her down the aisle. She will kiss his cheek and fumble through a graying beard, with her eyes on the future. She might move away and he will only see her on holidays. And when she says goodbye to him for the last time, and he is laid to rest, one thing will never change. She will always be his little girl, and he will *always* be her daddy.

The Gospel is relationship. The Gospel of our LORD Jesus Christ is that we have relationship with Jesus and his father.

> *"But now in Christ Jesus you who once were far off have been brought near by the blood of Christ. For he himself is our peace, who has made us both one and has broken down in his flesh the dividing wall of hostility by abolishing the law of commandments*

expressed in ordinances, that he might create in himself one new man in place of the two, so making peace, and might reconcile us both to God in one body through the cross, thereby killing the hostility. And he came and preached peace to you who were far off and peace to those who were near. For through him we both have access in one Spirit to the Father. So then you are no longer strangers and aliens, but you are fellow citizens with the saints and members of the household of God."

—Ephesians 2:13–19

The relationship never changes. Jesus frames our relationship with God as family. As Father to children, one of the best aspects is that no matter what season of life we are in, no matter what the circumstance or rhythm of the relationship at the time, we are always his children. We are still his beloved children, whether we thank him for the special moments or just go on with our day. Whether we spend copious hours in prayer, Bible study, volunteering or worship, or whether we are swept into the currents of our culture and forget to call Dad this week, month, or decade. We are still his beloved children.

At this point in your spiritual journey, you might be questioning my assertions. "Well, what about if you don't live a Christian life and you neglect God?" This question lives on a spectrum, so let's take it to its furthest conclusion: "What if you openly reject God?" Does the Father's love change?

"Who shall separate us from the love of Christ? Shall tribulation, or distress, or persecution, or famine, or nakedness, or danger, or sword? As it is written, "For your sake we are being killed all the day long; we are regarded as sheep to be slaughtered." No, in all these things we are more than conquerors through him who loved us. For I am sure that neither death nor life, nor angels

*nor rulers, nor things present nor things to come, nor powers, nor
height nor depth, nor anything else in all creation, will be able to
separate us from the love of God in Christ Jesus our LORD."*

—Romans 8:35–39

When you hear the Gospel and immediately look to validate it
by actions and intentions, I hope a warning siren goes off in your head
because you are confusing the Law and the Gospel. The Law says actions
and intentions, and the Gospel says relationship and reception. Sin,
death, and the devil want you to turn the Gospel into a law, thereby
removing love from the relationship and making it a contractual
obligation. If the man at the coffee house was contractually obligated
to provide the girl with a chocolate-sprinkle donut, they've lost the love.
Without love, there is no security. Without security, there is neither
trust nor faithfulness, and the relationship is at best an appeasing facade.
When love is present, the foundation of the relationship comes from the
faithfulness of the father, which creates a deep security and trust abiding
in the child. There is nothing you can do, or not do. Say or not say. Be or
not be. He will always be Dad.

In my first week of college, I met two men: Jeff and Scott. These
men told me about the relationship they had with God and how they
would meet each morning at 6 :00 a.m. at Panera Bread to study the
Bible and pray together. Jeff told me how this morning ritual had
become a cornerstone of his life, as it set the tone for the rest of his day. I
thought that was pretty cool but simultaneously thought that 6:00 a.m.
was really early. Scott invited me to come with them in the mornings,
so I said I would try to get there once in a while. Something stirred in
me over the next couple of days, and the Spirit drove me to find Scott
and tell him I would be there the next morning. I remember we looked
at John chapter 4, the story of Jesus and the woman of Samaria, and we

studied and cross-referenced and checked definitions. Scott showed me when Jacob dug the well in Genesis and how Moses later brought Israel to the mountains Gerizim and Ebal and how that story related to what we were reading in John. I was so astonished that a drive started within me to search, study, and learn the Bible.

For the first month of school, I spent on average three hours each day at Panera reading and studying. Unfortunately, all the time spent in scripture resulted in not spending any time on school work. After a month, I was failing two classes and marginally passing the rest. I had to stop going to Panera and get serious about getting my grades up.

It's been almost fifteen years, and I have gone through several seasons of intense study followed by absence, though I've never gone back to reading three hours a day. The Law will point out Joshua 1:8: *"Do not let this book of the Law depart from your mouths, meditate on it day and night so that you may be careful to do everything written in it, then you will be prosperous and successful."* The Law might remind me that I have never gotten back to that point in my life, like the saying, " 'Do this' and it's never done," but the Holy Spirit reminds me that no matter what, he is still Dad, and that is a comforting thing.

> *"For all who are led by the Spirit of God are sons of God. For you did not receive the spirit of slavery to fall back into fear, but you have received the Spirit of adoption as sons, by whom we cry, 'Abba! Father!' The Spirit himself bears witness with our spirit that we are children of God, and if children, then heirs—heirs of God and fellow heirs with Christ, provided we suffer with him in order that we may also be glorified with him."*

—Romans 8:14–17

THE MARKS OF THE GOSPEL

The Law just makes demands, while the Gospel makes a single demand and simultaneously provides its fulfillment. In other words, Jesus requires faith for salvation and at the same time gives that faith. This is a precious gift.

> *"I therefore, a prisoner for the LORD, urge you to walk in a manner worthy of the calling to which you have been called, with all humility and gentleness, with patience, bearing with one another in love, eager to maintain the unity of the Spirit in the bond of peace. There is one body and one Spirit just as you were called to the one hope that belongs to your call— one LORD, one faith, one baptism, one God and Father of all, who is over all and through all and in all. But grace was given to each one of us according to the measure of Christ's gift. Therefore it says, 'When he ascended on high he led a host of captives, and he gave gifts to men.'"*

—Ephesians 4:1–8

Paul is urging the church towards a selfless culture in their faith community. He wants the church to consider the unity that has been achieved by the Holy Spirit as we are bound together. To emphasize this command, Paul then points out the singular unity in the Gospel as we are brought into one faith community by the Holy Spirit. We are united with Jesus as the only LORD, brought into one faith by one baptism and bound to the Father through it all. Could you ever produce a faith worthy of the holiness of God? This is where one of my favorite sayings comes into play: "It's not about you." Oh how sin hates to hear that! This is the joy of the Gospel Paul describes. The faith necessary to bring us into salvation does not have its origin with us. It, like the Gospel, is focused solely on God: *"...looking to Jesus, the founder and perfecter of our faith"* (Hebrews 12:2a). Consider this as you are reading. The Gospel is like your copy of this book. If you're super anal, you could possibly produce a receipt to confirm that it's your book. And while it is your book, it is also my book. Its origin is with me sitting here writing the words, and yet it is distinctly yours. When Jesus was born of the Virgin Mary and made man through his life, he established the faith sufficient for salvation built on his obedience through suffering. *"Although he was a son, he learned obedience through what he suffered. And being made perfect, he became the source of eternal salvation to all who obey him"* (Hebrews 5:8–9). The faith necessary for salvation has its origin in Christ and, by a miracle of the Holy Spirit, is also distinctly ours. The Gospel is all this.

The Gospel of Jesus Christ simultaneously demands and provides faith. It brings us into the new covenant in Christ's blood that washes our sins and establishes a new relationship with God. The Law says sinner—the Gospel says saint. Therefore, the Gospel never attempts to correct the sinner, for there is no sinner left in it. In fact, the Gospel instantaneously, as it is proclaimed by the Holy Spirit, removes all fear, disappointment, regret, and guilt. The Gospel declares us a new creation! The old is gone; the new has come (2 Corinthians 5:17). We are the redeemed, saints washed in the blood of the Lamb! The Gospel treats us as 100% saint. Every and all requirements for contrition and discipline were fulfilled by Jesus and are therefore no longer our burden. If you find yourself holding on to guilt, you are confusing the Gospel with Law. Solution: Paul says in 1 Corinthians 6:20 and 7:23 *"you were bought with a price."* So consider the cost Jesus paid to satisfy the Law, to cover your sin, and win you for himself. You are not your own. Jesus through blood, sweat, and death has bought your sin. He owns it. So can you say, "I still need to carry the weight of it"? This question implies that you still need to feel guilty. To suggest it is to basically tell Jesus that his death wasn't enough. The truth is that Jesus takes your guilt and replaces it with repentance (a heart and mind towards God), which in the Gospel brings us to joy and hope at the promise of Christ's victory and our salvation.

The Gospel declares us saints, but that does not require anything saintly from us. We do not have to have a saintly heart or disposition. It does not require that we build upon the goodness that the Holy Spirit "got started." The Holy Spirit does not set us at the base of Mount Horeb and tell us to keep climbing until we reach God. It does not expect us to somehow produce a visible love for God or each other. The Gospel says abide, and it changes us. This is most evident in Jesus' teachings the night of his arrest.

It is a common confusion of the Law and Gospel to read Law statements in the New Testament as Gospel. Paul makes regular use of the Law in his teaching to the early churches. The confusion happens when we look at what Paul is teaching from a Gospel stance with our Law lenses on. So, we hear, "If we are Christians, then we ought to _____." When we work that logic backwards, our actions prove we are not Christians, and all hope and joy are gone. Instead, read it through the lens of the Law: "God says, we should _____," and our inability to do that forces us to look to Jesus for salvation. Your next challenge is to read from a Gospel perspective with a Gospel lens: "We are Christians, therefore the Holy Spirit has made us _____."

Wrong = If we are Christians, then we ought to be generous.

Right = We are Christians, therefore the Holy Spirit has made us generous.

We look at the opportunity to be generous not as an obligation but as natural as eating donuts (If you're like me). So read the encouragement and teaching of Paul from both perspectives, the Law allowing you to examine yourself and to discover your need for a savior, and the Gospel as your Savior accomplishing all this on your behalf, and the Spirit who has renewed you. As you practice this distinction, you will find the liberty of the Gospel. As Jesus says, *"Take my yoke upon you, and learn from me, for I am gentle and lowly in heart, and you will find rest for your souls. For my yoke is easy, and my burden is light"* (Matthew 11:29–30).

TAKEAWAYS

GOD'S LOVE: Your creator loves you. This truth is at the bedrock of your very being and is the foundation for your relationship with God, as he gave his only Son to save you.

MISCONCEPTIONS: Sin, death, and the devil want you to turn the Gospel into a law, thereby removing love from the relationship and making it a contractual obligation.

Sin, death, and the devil want you to regard the Law as irrelevant, thereby removing its purpose: to point you to Christ. In our attempt to err on the side of grace, we actually subvert the Law by creating no need for it.

GOD'S GIFTS: The Law allows you to examine yourself and to discover your need for a savior. The Gospel, your Savior, has accomplished all this on your behalf, and the Spirit has renewed you.

ACTION POINT: Start by listening for Gospel words and Law words. Then ask yourself, "Are they using those words to talk about the right thing, or are they switching them (e.g., using Gospel words to talk about the Law)?" A great way to figure it out is to check your feelings. Ask yourself: Does what is being said make me feel convicted, or does it make me want to despair? Does it lift me up and give me hope in Jesus? Developing that skill will help you learn to correctly use these tools in the right circumstances.

CHAPTER 13

Life as a Christian

THE NUMBER ONE REASON JESUS DIED ON THE CROSS

What is the number one reason Jesus died on the cross? (Pause and answer that question for yourself before you read on.) To save us from our sins. This is the number one answer but not the number one reason. We have a deep need to make things about us. (Remember the first lie of sin?) We like the idea of the Gospel being about *our* salvation, Jesus dying for *us* and *our* reception of it. Do you remember the parable of the Prodigal Son? Luke chronicles a parable Jesus taught in Luke 15:11ff about a man who had two sons. The younger son cashed in his inheritance and squandered it on foolish living. The older son rebuked the father's lavish reception of the younger son's humble return. This story, like most of the parables, teaches the Gospel. The problem is we always make it about us. We look at the younger and older son and extract all kinds of application for ourselves. The truth is that the parable titled "Prodigal

Son" isn't about the sons at all. It's about the Father: the Father's lavish love of the younger son and faithful love of the elder. It's about how the father humiliates himself to run after his lost boy and then leaves the banquet to teach his indignant heir.

The number one reason Jesus died on the cross is this: to fulfill the will of his Father. Before Jesus' arrest, all three Synoptic Gospels recount Jesus praying, "Father take this cup from me, but not my will but yours be done."[16] *"Yet it was the will of the LORD to crush him; he has put him to grief; when his soul makes an offering for guilt, he shall see his offspring; he shall prolong his days; the will of the LORD shall prosper in his hand"* (Isaiah 53:10). John recounts that evening, adding other details like the washing of the disciples' feet. Jesus takes off his outer garment, wraps a towel around his waist, and washes their feet. But we miss the beginning of that scene: *"Jesus, knowing that **the Father** had given all things into his hands, and that he had come **from God** and was going back **to God"*** (John 13:3). So, Jesus serves his disciples. However, we miss that for the part about us.

Jesus prays hours before his crucifixion asking the Father if there is any other way this can be done. The cost of our salvation is the death of God. Jesus, who is life, had to die. This is the only time Jesus has ever been separated from the Father. Jesus loves us with the same love as the Father, but the cost of our salvation was a lot to bear—he sweat blood. So, he is looking for a way out, a way out of the cost of our redemption, but not a way out of God's will. If there had been any other way, Jesus would have preferred it, but not at the cost of his Father's will. Is it true that Jesus died on the cross because he loves us and wants us back? *Of course!* But even his own love is a secondary motivation. Jesus is supremely interested in the will of the Father, and everything else is second to it. We must not only submit to this truth but rejoice in it. It is in his perfect obedience to the will of the Father that he established a righteousness worthy of the LORD's holiness for us to receive through faith. [17] In simple words, it is Jesus' perfect completion of the Father's will that achieved our righteousness. At Jesus' coronation after the ascension, an Elder tells John to stop wailing because the Lion of the tribe of Judah, the Root of David, has conquered death and is able to unleash the will of God in the end. What has qualified him for this?

> *"And they sang a new song, 'Worthy are you to take the scroll and to open its seals, for you were slain, and by your blood you ransomed people **for God** from every tribe and language and people and nation, and you have made them a kingdom and priests **to our God**, and they shall reign on the earth.'"*

—Revelation 5:9–10

We come back to that simple saying: *"It's not about you."* This is most certainly true of the Gospel. Jesus is not a shy, brainy teen with a massive crush on the quarterback who constantly abuses that affection by getting Jesus to write his papers. If we think Jesus' number one reason to die on the cross is to achieve our salvation, it makes Jesus seem like that teen: always giving, never getting, a doormat for our feet. Then the focus is on us, and we have to make a choice to treat that doormat with respect. Now that might be easy for you, if that doormat is a family heirloom you've seen in the homes of your heritage. So you take off your shoes before you walk on it, and you place it at the side of your bed and kneel on it to pray every night. You don't think anything of the behavior because you were raised on it, but to the observer, it's just a doormat, of little consequence and easily overlooked or disregarded. You don't think the quarterback has a host of nerds happy to write his papers? The power of the Gospel has been sacrificed for the self-satisfied. When we place the value of the Gospel on ourselves, we sacrifice a worthy Savior. Is a doormat worthy of praise and adoration? Is the brainy teen worthy of our submission? Do you want to follow him?

Now what about a Jesus who is willing to endure the shame, ridicule, pain, and suffering to accomplish a purpose greater than the quarterback's? What if Jesus is writing our papers, passing our classes, not because we are worth it, but because he is serving a greater purpose?

Do you remember Chris Nolan's *The Dark Knight*, the second of his Batman trilogy? If you haven't seen it, watch it because I'm about to spoil it (sorry). At the end, all of Gotham's hopes have been lost because Harvey Dent loses his mind and goes on a killing spree. Batman, the misunderstood vigilante stops Harvey from killing the son of Commissioner Gordon and in the process kills Dent. If the world finds out what Harvey did, everything would be lost. So Batman, in that terrible growly voice, tells Gordon, "I killed those people; that's what I can be." Gordon rejects the idea, exclaiming that Batman can't take responsibility for Dent's actions. "I'm whatever Gotham needs me to be," Batman responds as he hands Gordon his radio and says, "Call it in." So, the police label Batman the killer of Harvey Dent and all the others lost at Harvey's hand, and he is no longer a friend to Gotham. They hunt him, they set the dogs on him, and they label him a murderer, all because he serves a greater purpose, "because sometimes the truth isn't good enough; sometimes people deserve to have their faith rewarded." Gordon's son says to his dad, "But he didn't do anything wrong." Gordon explains, "He's the hero Gotham deserves, but not the one it needs right now. So we'll hunt him, because he can take it, because he's not our hero. He's a silent guardian, a watchful protector. A Dark Knight."

Yep, I cry every time because Nolan has told the story of a hero worthy of honor. He does what no one else can do. No matter how it looks on the outside, his character and conviction runs deep. Jesus is the Dark Knight; he doesn't come to stop the Romans or lead some magisterial reform that sets God's people to a prosperous future. He is more: he pays the penalty of sin and achieves a holiness worthy of the Almighty for all creation. We never ask for it; we never deserve it.

In fact, we spend most of our waking hours rejecting and ridiculing it. But through the shame, humility, jeers, spit, and the shouts to crucify the traitor, Jesus never wavers in his conviction. He will accomplish the Father's will. So he endures, he holds fast, even to his own death. And he is someone worth following. He is someone worthy of our admiration and praise, someone we can be proud to serve. This is the power of the Gospel.

> *"For I am not ashamed of the gospel, for it is the power of God for salvation to everyone who believes, to the Jew first and also to the Greek."*

—Romans 1:16

> *"For the word of the cross is folly to those who are perishing, but to us who are being saved it is the power of God."*

—1 Corinthians 1:18

HOW DO WE RELATE TO GOD?

We must agree that the Gospel is about Jesus: Jesus' submission to the Father and Jesus' acquisition by his blood of people from every tribe, language, and nation for God. Every sentence concerning the Gospel must have at its focus Jesus. It is not a Gospel statement to say, "Jesus died to save *me* from my sins" if the emphasis is on you, your salvation. This is a gray space where sin, death, and the devil often play. If the focus is on Jesus' sacrifice, the cost of my salvation, then it's a true Gospel statement. Yet with the same words, sin can twist our minds and hearts to make us think it's all about us. So you must be on guard to observe this truth: anytime the focus is leaving Jesus and going to someone or something else, alarms should ring in your head, "You are now leaving the Gospel." The Gospel is *all about Jesus*. There is no truer or simpler statement. It is. Period. Anything that diminishes this truth, or confuses it, does not hold the Gospel. *"He must increase, I must decrease"* (John 3:30).

In college I spent lots of time having conversations with other Christians about faith and the contents of its teaching. Nine times out of ten those conversations always came down to the same topic—how do we relate to God? This is the most fundamental Gospel question which holds the power of the Gospel, the origin of faith, and the mission of the Church.

Do we choose God or does God choose us? The two options are libertarian free will and compatibilist free will. Libertarian free will is the position held by many Christians (though globally the minority) that says we choose God. Libertarian free will is held on a spectrum, with the complete freedom to choose on one side, and needing *a lot* of help from the Holy Spirit on the other, but at the end of the day you still have to pull the trigger and make the choice.

Compatibilist free will is the other option and is easiest explained in a metaphor. (Now I picture Gandalf in front of three doorways trying to choose which way to go forward in the Mines of Moria, but if you aren't quite the nerd I am, fill in your own picture.) If your only option is to go forward, and there are three doors in front of you—A, B, and C—how many options do you have to proceed? Three, right? What if door B is a hidden door that you have absolutely no knowledge of? How many options to proceed do you have? Two, because you are unaware of all the options. Compatibilist free will says we have freedom to choose options compatible with ourselves. So I can choose to live in the desert, or the mountains, but not underwater or in space (without technical support). I can choose to watch professional baseball, but I cannot choose to play it. I can choose to reject God because I myself am a sinner, but I cannot choose to be holy because I myself am not capable of perfection. This means God must choose me because I cannot make that decision for myself. Consider your own feelings. Neither of these systems completely depicts the nature of our freedom, and both are described in the scriptures. But I myself choose to ascribe to theology that emphasizes the one truth: The Gospel is about Jesus. Which of these two free wills emphasizes Jesus' work more? Which one ultimately focuses on us? Is the good news that I choose Jesus, or that Jesus chooses me?

Some will suggest that libertarian free will is the choice to receive. I've heard the analogy of being offered a completely free luxury European car to replace my 2000 Buick LeSabre. It's like the Holy Spirit is putting the keys in my hand and saying, "Just take it." All I have to do is call it my own. But even still, it comes down to my acceptance of the gift. It does emphasize the worth of the gift, and my complete unworthiness of it, but the focus is on me and what I will do. Don't be tricked. In this metaphor, the compatibilist perspective makes more real-world sense. I'm picturing someone walking into this coffee shop and handing me keys to a Ferrari parked outside. I'm confused by the gesture, even after long explanations of what is happening. I don't believe it; it doesn't make sense; I'm wondering if it's stolen. Even in my own analogy I know it's not stolen, and it's for me, but I can't really take the keys because it doesn't make sense—it's not my car. And I'm waiting to find out the truth behind the interaction. My reality doesn't jive with that hypothetical. I can't make it work in my world. The power of the Gospel is in Jesus' completion of the will of the Father, in choosing to redeem us with his blood. It is also the full demonstration of the Father's love.

"For while we were still weak, at the right time Christ died for the ungodly. For one will scarcely die for a righteous person— though perhaps for a good person one would dare even to die but God shows his love for us in that while we were still sinners,

Christ died for us. Since, therefore, we have now been justified by his blood, much more shall we be saved by him from the wrath of God. For if while we were enemies we were reconciled to God by the death of his Son, much more, now that we are reconciled, shall we be saved by his life. More than that, we also rejoice in God through our LORD Jesus Christ, through whom we have now received reconciliation."

—Romans 5:6–11

In the first verses of Romans 5, Paul describes the hope of salvation we have through faith in the grace of Jesus by the Holy Spirit. If the hope of our salvation is founded on us, our choosing to agree to the acceptance of the reception of this free gift of Jesus (hyperbole intended) results in no real hope, because as quickly as we accept Jesus, we can reject him. If salvation is contingent on our faithfulness to his faithfulness, we have much despair indeed. For when have I ever been consistent? Steadfast? What if at the end of my life, in moments of suffering and grief, I lose grasp of faith? Will a life of faithfulness be null and void? (And so quickly the word of the Gospel has been confused with works of the Law.) In my suffering, if I am incapable of receiving faith because I am overwhelmed with pain, am I outside the reach of the Gospel? What of those individuals who have intellectual or cognitive disabilities from injury or from birth? If they don't have the capacity to accept, are they outside the reach of the Gospel? Maybe you will argue that people born with disabilities that make them unable to profess faith are in some way on a different playing field. Innocent before God. If that's true, and their innocence excludes them from needing to accept Jesus, then only two options are available. Either they are outside of Jesus' salvation because of their innocence, or the Holy Spirit made the choice for them—and if that's the case, whose salvation is more secure? The one held by the Holy

Spirit, or the one who chooses? And if there are multiple ways to receive faith, then which one is preferable and therefore more generous? I can't even find the Gospel in this line of thought.

Paul says we have been justified by faith, which brings us peace with God through Jesus. We have passively been saved by means of faith. While we were weak and ungodly, it was done for us, not by us. One of my favorite displays of the Gospel is when we receive the Lord's Supper. Most of the congregation comes to the front of the church, presents themselves, kneels, opens their hands, bows, receives, and heads back to their seats. But that's not my favorite. It's my blue hairs, the ones with the walkers who now sit in the back of the church because they don't have the stamina to get to their former pews. So, they take up residence in the back of the sanctuary, unable to come forward and practice the Lord's Supper like they did for decades. But they don't miss out. In fact, the forgiveness of Jesus in his body and blood leave the altar and come to the back of the sanctuary. They don't stand, or kneel; only their heads bow, and Jesus meets them there and forgives their sins too.

If the Gospel is about Jesus redeeming people for God, and he is capable of redeeming all people no matter their circumstance, does this also apply to children, even infants? I love doing adult baptisms, but children hold a special place in my heart because they didn't ask for faith, nor did they decide to come forward. They aren't even capable of coming forward. They must be brought, like the paralyzed man through the roof.[18] And Jesus meets them at the water and washes them without their knowledge or understanding. Jesus brings love to the old, the weak, the wretched, the winner, the disabled, and the child at the same place while they are still sinners. We are justified, reconciled, and saved all passively according to Paul.[19] This means no matter where you are in your life, no matter how alone or lost you are or have been, no matter your decisions, your failures, or your success, Jesus will meet you where you are and bring you to himself. This is the Gospel that cannot be kept silent but must be proclaimed. Jesus has won! Even the rocks will cry out! *"For what we proclaim is not ourselves, but Jesus Christ as Lord, with ourselves as your servants for Jesus' sake"* (2 Corinthians 4:5).

CHAPTER 14

The Rhythm of Life in Christ

The Gospel: Jesus, by his blood, ransomed people for God from every tribe, tongue, and nation and has made them a kingdom of priests to our God.

The focus is all on Jesus: his work, his suffering and death, his resurrection and ascension. So, what is left for us? How do we respond? Language gets very tricky here because we want to make sure that as we talk about the Gospel, we don't make it about ourselves. Our sinful nature constantly works against us by trying to get us to make the Gospel about us. So we must always strive to die to ourselves. *"I have been crucified with Christ. It is no longer I who live, but Christ who lives in me. And the life I now live in the flesh I live by faith in the Son of God, who loved me and gave himself for me"* (Galatians 2:20). This passage brings up this question: How we are to live in the Gospel of Jesus?

In his gospel, John recounts the story of the Last Supper in John 13. Jesus, in view of his purpose and relationship to the Father, washes the disciples' feet before the meal.[20] Judas leaves to betray Jesus later, and Jesus begins teaching his disciples for the last time. In John 13:31 through chapter 17, John chronicles those last teachings before Jesus' Passion. In chapter 18 John says the group went out to the Garden of Gethsemane, so this teaching had to have happened in the Upper Room at the close of the meal or while they were walking. I picture the disciples sitting in the Upper Room as Jesus spends this intentional and focused time with his students, answering their many questions where everyone is perfectly exposed. No one can dangle at the back of the pack. Each has to wrestle with what Jesus is saying. There are a couple threads that weave throughout his teachings in this chapter, and the first and foremost is God's (the Father) glory.[21] The Father and the Son's glory is intertwined. The glory of the Father is displayed in the work of the Son: *"I glorified you on earth, having accomplished the work that you gave me to do"* (John 17:4). And in turn, the Father endorses the saving death and resurrection of the Son by affirming the Son's pre-incarnate glory.[22]

If that is all over your head, don't worry. The key is that the Father's glory is directly linked to the Gospel of Jesus the Christ. He calls his disciples to believe,[23] abide,[24] and love.[25] In this teaching, Jesus connects the Father's glory to his ministry as it pertains to his disciples, and it is this point that brings clarity to how we live as Christians, followers, and fellow disciples of Jesus. He gives three imperatives to his disciples. First, love one another: *"By this all people will know that you are my disciples, if you have love for one another"* (John 13:34–35). Second, ask, in his name (John 14:13, 15:7) and third, bear much fruit (John 15:8). Take caution, as it is easy to take these imperatives and try to make them about us, our actions, and our decisions.

CHAPTER FOURTEEN

ABIDE: STAY IN HIS CORNER

John 15 brings all of Jesus' teaching for this last session into focus. He uses the metaphor of a vine and its branches to describe how we (the branches) live in Jesus (the vine). Two words rise to focus in verses 1–17: fruit and abide. It makes sense that we focus on fruit. After all, everyone knows the focus of a vineyard is on the fruit produced. Our attention focuses on verses 2, 5, and 8.

> *"Every branch in me that does not bear fruit he takes away, and every branch that does bear fruit he prunes, that it may bear more fruit."*

—John 15:2

> *"I am the vine; you are the branches. Whoever abides in me and I in him, he it is that bears much fruit, for apart from me you can do nothing."*

—John 15:5

> *"By this my Father is glorified, that you bear much fruit and so prove to be my disciples."*

—John 15:8

Our attention always goes to the things that matter to us. Usually it's the things we think we can influence. We desire to prove our devotion to God, to ourselves, and sometimes to others, so we study Jesus' teaching and discover that the fruit he desires is that we love one another.[26] Then we go looking for the resources we need to produce this fruit. The most devout (or anyone who can read verse 5) will agree that we can't produce the fruit on our own, but we still think that we somehow do the work. Consequently, the Christian life becomes a rhythm of trying to tap into divine power in order to prove ourselves. The more Christian disciplines we master (prayer, Bible study, service, evangelism, etc.), the more we validate our and others' devotion.

We seem to spend a lot of time measuring ourselves and others by the works we do and the works we think we do. We store up in ourselves all kinds of ideas about how good a producer we are. If not in action, hey, it's the thought that counts!

We hear the promise of Jesus in verse 7 and 8 that we can ask for whatever we wish and it will be done for us. We get crazy ideas about what that means. Ask whatever you wish? I can wish for some pretty big stuff there, Jesus. I'm thinking the Batmobile from the first Batman movie with Michael Keaton where you say, "Shields," and it all locks up. That would be pretty cool. And it's true we can ask God for whatever we want, big or small, but this idea gets really dangerous when we tag it to the next verse in this line of thought. The Father is glorified in our bearing of fruit which "proves" us to be disciples. So God, if you want everyone to know how good the fruit is that I produce, and how faithful you are to my ministry, then you should probably get me a Batmobile. And why don't you just put "Faithful Follower" on the license plate or "St Luke's Pastor" so everyone knows how special I am? I mean humble... that's the fruit...sorry, I meant humble.

Mac Davis wrote a song, "It's Hard to Be Humble." But if I'm honest, and take a real inventory of myself, it actually becomes quite simple to be humble because I really don't have much fruit to speak of in the way of righteousness. Not my own. If we were able to complete the Law of God and love him and others completely, then this system would work perfectly. But you know as well as I do that we don't love others nearly as well as we want to. At our best the desire is on our heart, which scarcely plays out the way we want. I drive home after work excited to spend time with my wife and children. I want to show them how much I love them with quality time together. But when I get home, my wife is exhausted from the kids who aren't listening today, and there's enough stuff that needs to get done that I get resentful because now I'll spend my evening working too. If we focus on the fruit, we only see the problem. The truth is that we can never love people enough to be able to validate Jesus' love in our lives. On front stage we can act however successful we want, but back stage we know a different story, one of fear, doubt, and unease. This is quite the opposite of Jesus' promises in Matthew 5, the Beatitudes. The libertarian free will always struggles with turning the Gospel into the Law, which is exactly what has happened here.

The Gospel tells a different story, as it sees a different focus for this teaching, which we skip over with a glance. *"Already you are clean because of the word that I have spoken to you"* (John 15:3). Jesus has washed us clean by his word. *"I am the way the truth and the life. No one comes to the Father except through me"* (John 14:6). You are grafted in with no work necessary because you are already his—the vinedresser. He has seen fit to bring you into the vine. As you read the stories of the Bible, you hear firsthand the word of Jesus and his faithfulness to that word. Don't let go of that. It's our identity in Jesus that is founded in his faithfulness. The Gospel teaches us to see what is truly important for us: abide. The word "abide" is said 11 times in just 17 verses; whereas fruit is only mentioned six times. To the layman, the metaphor about a vineyard focuses on fruit, but to the vinedresser, it's about the vine. It is the vine that produces the fruit; it is the vine that is responsible for the character and taste spectrum of the grape. Branches come and go in their seasons, but the vine ever remains. Vineyards today trace the origin of their vines back through centuries and across continents. We like to make it about the branch, but it's about the vine. The vinedresser looking to produce fruit goes to the vine with branches. It's his most trusted vine which has been faithful throughout all generations, a good vine, producing good fruit in and out of season. We need not worry about the fruit produced through us because that is the responsibility of the vine, not us. It's the vine's responsibility, and it's our joy. To abide and witness fruit produced in your life brings you joy and praise to the Father and Jesus, for it is their work, not ours.[27]

> "As the Father has loved me, so have I loved you. Abide in my love. If you keep my commandments, you will abide in my love, just as I have kept my Father's commandments and abide in his love. These things I have spoken to you, that my joy may be in you, and that your joy may be full."

—John 15:9–11

We look to have our eyes opened, to wait on the LORD, to watch for his hand. We pray, asking God to help us abide fully and continually so that he will always be nurturing us and pruning us because it brings our joy. Like King David's 24/7 prayer:

> "One thing have I asked of the LORD, that will I seek after: that I may dwell in the house of the LORD all the days of my life, to gaze upon the beauty of the LORD and to inquire in his temple."

—Psalm 27:4

At this point, sin likes to play a witty trick on us. As soon as we get comfortable, we try to take control. Jesus teaches the disciples to just stay in their corner. I've never watched any real boxing, but I love the *Rocky* movies. What I don't understand about boxing is: Why would you ever leave the corner? When you're in the corner you're getting toweled off, rubbed down, and sprayed with water while someone shouts all kinds of encouraging words to you like, "You got this! Watch out for that! You can win this!" The bell dings, you get up, and go back into the ring, where you get punched in the face (Apollo Creed doesn't look like the kind of guy who punches soft). If you're like me, and I know I am, I don't like to get punched in the face. In this chapter Jesus is saying that no matter the round, never leave your corner because in your corner I'm coaching and encouraging you, reminding you of your training and the work I'm doing in and through you. But don't be confused. Jesus isn't Mickey, and you're not Rocky. Jesus is Rocky. And when the bell rings, he steps through the ropes and walks out into the ring for you. Rocky doesn't go toe-to-toe with Apollo thinking he's the better fighter. Rocky sees the road to victory and takes a wicked beating. Round after round he keeps getting back up, because he isn't going to lose your fight. When the last bell rings and sin and death are on the canvas, he grabs your hand and raises it to the sky. This is your victory, your joy.

It's so easy for us to skip over these verses to look for fruit. But the teaching in this chapter isn't about producing fruit. It's about abiding, because without abiding we've lost everything. Don't confuse abiding with fruit. Abiding isn't about doing something to stay tapped in. Abiding isn't a "doing"—it's a "being," and Jesus is clear about where that being starts. The challenge is always to abide. Let Rocky do your fighting.

WHAT ABOUT FRUIT?

As Jesus' teaching focuses on abiding, it is in the natural condition of that abiding that we produce fruit. What is it that Jesus is referring to when he talks about fruit? It's not church discipline, and it's not good deeds. Neither of these glorify the Father in and of themselves. Jesus says, however, that the bearing of this fruit is proof of being a student of Jesus and is to the glory of the Father.

"By this my Father is glorified, that you bear much fruit and so prove to be my disciples."

—John 15:8

"A new commandment I give to you, that you love one another: just as I have loved you, you also are to love one another. By this all people will know that you are my disciples, if you have love for one another."

—John 13:34–35

"If you keep my commandments, you will abide in my love, just as I have kept my Father's commandments and abide in his love."

—John 15:10

We are to love one another. Such fear of failure surrounds the idea of fruit, until love comes into view. Love is the foundation of freedom and liberation. Love produces a joy that is eternal and unchanging. It brings peace through tumult and hope through the impossible. It is freeing and yet completely tethered unless we limit love to discipline or good deeds. Do you "prove" your love? Did you get a card in the mail early enough that it arrives before the big event? Did you make your phone call the morning of their birthday? Are you planning to treat your mother to something special on Mother's Day so that she "knows" how much you love her? If your love turns into actions, then this reads as a way of earning Jesus' and the Father's love, and you quickly discover that the promise of the next verse, "full joy," is unattainable. This also means that if you have no joy, you're probably loving the wrong things.

If you have no joy in your marriage, you're probably loving the wrong things. If you have no joy in your labors, you're probably loving the wrong things. If you have no joy in your church, you're probably loving the wrong things. The national message of evangelical Christianity in America, as recorded in the media, is missing the love. I wonder if it loves Church tradition and God's Law more than people. It preaches love of self-validation over sacrificial service. As we read the gospels, the Church today has a lot in common with the Pharisees.

THERE ARE TWO HUGE PROMISES IN THIS CHAPTER...

"If you abide in me, and my words abide in you, ask whatever you wish, and it will be done for you."

—John 15:7

"These things I have spoken to you, that my joy may be in you, and that your joy may be full."

—John 15:11

The commandment "Love one another" is the fruit produced through us. Love is simultaneously action and condition. It is a relationship as much as it is relational, which means it is being as much as it is doing. Now we can read these promises with context. No matter the season of life, you always abide because you've been grafted into a good vine by a loving Father. The Father is glorified because you have confidence and full access in Jesus to ask for whatever you wish. That's a blank check that doesn't lead to riches or fame, which are just toys and trinkets. I've sat with many people at the last season of their life and have never heard them tell me they wanted more things or fame. They want more time with the people they love because in that love they found joy. Ask for what he promises to give, that you abide in his love, and that his love extends through you to the people around you—that's where joy lives. That is the fruit he is producing through you. Don't settle for the lie that counts how much and how often you pray and read your Bible, or how often you do the right things instead of the wrong things or whether you sign up for the service day or not. He is still your Father, and Jesus your Savior. That relationship is never going to change. Appreciate every season of the journey. Call to mind the great love he has for you.

Up to this point in your faith journey, if joy has been elusive and you find yourself trying to perform for someone (Jesus, yourself, or the church), I want you to close your eyes and quiet your heart and mind about all the things you think make up a Christian life. Just be still and consider how Jesus has loved you. What has he done to win love for you and fill you with his love? Think of all the promises he has made to you and the wrongs he's carried for you. Think of all the good he has brought you and all the loves he's brought into your life. Now tell me. Are you thinking of those people you love? What do you wish for them truly, above all else, for their lives? Ask God for it. Ask whatever you wish, and it will be done for you. Open your eyes. Joy.

THE WORK OF THE HOLY SPIRIT

The key to the whole thing is love. Christ is showing us the full extent of his love as he brings many brothers and sisters to righteousness.[28] So we focus on how Christ brings us into his love, what that love is capable of, and how it flows through us into loving others. This is still kind of a tall order, especially when you consider that Jesus is saying it one moment, doing it the next, and then leaving. They say absence makes the heart grow fonder. I say absence makes it easier to wonder. Now, my wife and I realize I am high maintenance—I don't pretend I'm not. I am always wondering about the extent of others' love for me. I'm not concerned with everyone, just those I hold close to my heart. Sin seizes my vulnerability and leads me to doubt and wonder. It makes me ineffective in the fruit department because I'm only concerned about myself. As soon as love isn't in front of my face, it makes it easier to wonder how real it is—how far it will go. That is the challenge with long distance relationships. I hope you aren't empathizing with what I'm saying in the sense of "my spouse is gone for the weekend, so I wonder if he/she loves me." That is a special kind of high maintenance, but consider how you might feel being separated for 10 months or 10 years. What about 30 years?

They call them military brats. They are raised on the notion that their father was away working to make a life for them because he loves them. But with only a few letters in hand, how easy is it to question whether his heart is really somewhere else? Those families sacrifice a lot for the rest of us and deserve our support.

We've logged 2,000 years since the time Jesus ascended. That's a long time to not be with someone. I guess that number doesn't really matter, but sometimes the question hits in your early teens, "What about his love?" During our teens, our parents' love doesn't seem to carry the same importance as the love of our peers either. Sometimes it hits in your 20s or 30s and you ask, "What about his love?" College professors have it all figured out. I have it all figured out, until I don't. Even in the twilight part of life, when loss and sometimes suffering are overwhelming, "What about his love?" When the unexpected makes you question what you've believed for so many years, or when sin throws a wrench in your life making it very easy to feel like a gulf separates you from his love, it's hard to read any joy or hope in chapter 15. "*Abide in my love.*" "*If you remain in me and my words remain in you, ask whatever you wish and it will be done for you."*

Jesus knew we needed help, so that's where the Helper comes in. If we seriously look at these first teachings, we realize we don't have a chance on our own. So Jesus immediately begins teaching about the Helper his Father would send to take care of us. Who is the Helper you might ask? Why, the Holy Spirit. Who is the Holy Spirit? Yeah, I get that a lot.

The Holy Spirit is the baritone of the acapella group. I know because that was my part. The tenor gets sweet high notes. The bass walks down the scales. The front man leads, and the baritone is—doo wop. Doberman...chewawawaa. The baritone is holding it down and keeping the group together. It's the most crucial part (though my example didn't really illustrate that point). Okay, I've belabored this metaphor and stood too long on my soap box.

The Holy Spirit's part isn't more crucial than the Father or the Son. It is just as critical because abiding is...well, hard. It's not something we are capable of, and it's the Holy Spirit who makes that happen. How is this for truth? Whether you know it or not, you abide in Jesus' love. You are never outside of it or removed from it. The Holy Spirit is the guarantee of that.

> *"When the Spirit of truth comes, he will guide you into all the truth, for he will not speak on his own authority, but whatever he hears he will speak, and he will declare to you the things that are to come."*

—John 16:13

So the Holy Spirit brings our lives into the Gospel of Jesus, and the Gospel of Jesus into our lives. He brings the faith Christ authored and perfected into our lives and makes it our own. And he reveals the fundamental truth of faith in three distinct ways: sin, righteousness, and judgment.

"Concerning sin, because they do not believe in me" (John 16:9). It's the Holy Spirit who reveals the bedrock of the fundamental truth of the faith. Sin is the reason people go to hell. In the New Covenant, by the blood of Jesus, sin is not doing or not doing; it's the lack of faith. There is nothing you can do that will ever separate you from the love of Jesus. You can never lose your faith. Yes, if it were up to you, faith, like your car keys, could easily be misplaced, but the Holy Spirit is the guarantee of that faith and its fortitude.

"Concerning righteousness, because I go to the Father, and you will see me no longer" (John 16:10). Jesus' current residence is often overlooked. He sits at the right hand of the Ancient of Days, the Alpha to Omega, Elohim, the Great I AM, and Jesus is putting all of his enemies under his footstool.[29] There is nothing that can stop him from accomplishing the Father's will in your redemption and salvation.[30] By the Holy Spirit, we who abide declare to all of our LORD Jesus' enemies—to sin, death, and the devil who try and assail us and separate us from the love of God in Jesus—with full confidence in faith, in the work of the Holy Spirit in our lives. *Where Christ is there I will be also. For he has risen above every rule and authority and has accomplished the will of the Father (see James 4:7).*

"Concerning judgment, because the ruler of this world is judged" (John 16:11). The Holy Spirit allows us to see what disobedience to the will of God is—it is judged and found wanting. The Holy Spirit enables us to be in the world but not of the world,[31] to sift through the garbage and see it for what it is. The Holy Spirit helps us know what parts of this life bring joy in love and what parts leave a bad taste in our mouths and a feeling of emptiness. Our Helper gives us clarity to see where love, joy, and hope are needed and shows us how God is utilizing us in that mission.

The Commission to Make Disciples

HERE I AM SEND ME

God has truly and graciously granted us all things. Now we move to the rhythm of abiding—how it looks and functions in our everyday lives. The second half of this book has been about abiding because to be, to abide, to dwell in the presence of God, brings us to a greater appreciation of his glory. Pause a moment to consider the blessings that abide. Isaiah, the most quoted prophet of the Old Testament by Jesus and Paul, recounts his commission to be prophet. The sixth chapter of Isaiah depicts the rhythm of abiding as a faithful follower and provides us with a great example we can study and apply to our own lives:

> *"In the year that King Uzziah died I saw the LORD sitting upon a throne, high and lifted up; and the train of his robe filled*

*the temple. Above him stood the seraphim. Each had six wings:
with two he covered his face, and with two he covered his feet, and
with two he flew. And one called to another and said: 'Holy, holy,
holy is the LORD of hosts; the whole earth is full of his glory!' And
the foundations of the thresholds shook at the voice of him who
called, and the house was filled with smoke."*

—Isaiah 6:1–4

Isaiah is in the presence of the LORD, and the train of his robe fills
the temple.

Have you seen Meghan Markle's wedding veil? It was 16.5 feet.
Notice, it wasn't as long as Kate's train, which was 25 feet, the same
length as Diana's. Just saying. What do you think the length of their
trains represented? How many weddings have you been to? How long
was the bride's train? Three to five feet? The train represents the glory
and majesty of the bride, the family, and the event they are celebrating.
Isaiah's vision depicts Adonai's train filling the temple. His glory is
revered by the six-winged creatures who were created for just this holy
purpose: to chant praises before Yahweh's throne, to raise the worship
of the heavenly host along with all creation. Then it says the house was
filled with smoke, to which Isaiah responds, *"Woe is me! For I am lost; for
I am a man of unclean lips, and I dwell in the midst of a people of unclean
lips; for my eyes have seen the King, the LORD of hosts!"* (Isaiah 6:5). Isaiah
responds this way because of what the smoke signals. In Hebrew, smoke
has the connotation of the herald of an enemy, the destruction of the
city, or the breath of a crocodile. (I like that last one.) In other words,
Isaiah was alarmed because this is a dangerous situation.

We like to think of loving "Easter Jesus" with lilies and butterflies.
We focus most of our attention on the love of God in Jesus (as we
should) but forget to consider his Holiness and the lengths he is willing

to go to maintain it. Isaiah is in the presence of God, and his response to God's holiness is "woe is me." The coronation of Jesus is depicted in John's Revelation in chapter 5, as it ushers in the metaphors about the seals. Most people recognize chapter 7 as it is a regular at memorial services: *"For the Lamb in the midst of the throne will be their shepherd, and he will guide them to springs of living water, and God will wipe away every tear from their eyes"* (Revelation 7:17). That follows nicely with our buddy Jesus image. But chapter 5 depicts a terrible situation in Heaven. The Father is holding a scroll and its seals must be opened to reveal the finale to God's redemptive plan. No one is holy enough. No one has accomplished God's will in righteousness and is therefore worthy to open its seals. This terrible fate brings John to weep bitterly. But the elder tells him, *"Weep no more; behold, the Lion of the tribe of Judah, the Root of David, has conquered, so that he can open the scroll and its seven seals"* (Revelation 5:5). And then we see a Lamb, *standing as though it had been slain,* who is worthy to take the scroll and open its seals.

I realize that Jesus will wipe away every tear from our eyes, but at the sight of the glory of the Lamb I believe we will weep, and weep bitterly, not out of fear but for what we have been spared. In view of God's mercy, his glory, and holiness, we repent. Repentance is the name given in scripture to the rhythm of abiding. Repentance is not about feeling guilty or sad about our sin; it's much more than that. It's about seeing God for who he is. When we finally consider ourselves in view of God, we realize our unworthiness. This is the root of humility and the heart of John the Baptist: *"He must increase, but I must decrease"* (John 3:30). It's true we will experience guilt and sadness for our sin as God's Law calls sin "sin" in our lives. But we also find forgiveness and confidence in the Gospel of our Savior as we are reminded we are good with God by the blood of Jesus. It gives us the confidence like Isaiah to confess our sins, "I am a person of unclean lips." The cost of abiding is the constant reminder of our unworthiness before God, but that belief makes us treasure the forgiveness Jesus won at Golgotha.

Repentance gives us full assurance that even as we confess our sin and have received forgiveness, we will also be consecrated righteous. Isaiah confesses his sins, *"Then one of the seraphim flew to [him], having in his hand a burning coal that he had taken with tongs from the altar. And he touched [Isaiah's] mouth and said: 'Behold, this has touched your lips; your guilt is taken away, and your sin atoned for'"* (Isaiah 6:6–7). Luckily, Isaiah provides the interpretation of the act in his account. His sin is symbolically covered and he is now qualified, qualified to stand in the presence of Adonai and to be privy to this strategic planning meeting. Confession leads to peace because we abide in the firm truth that Jesus has atoned for our sins, and in his grace we belong in the presence of the Ancient of Days. We are whole, holy, and consecrated.

After sin has been dealt with, the conversation continues. *"And I heard the voice of the LORD saying, 'Whom shall I send, and who will go for us?' Then I said, 'Here I am! Send me'"* (Isaiah 6:8). I love the change that has happened in Isaiah. One moment he is immobilized by fear; the next moment he's a fervent servant. He cries out to the heavenly host before the throne of God, *"Here I am! Send me!"* As we abide in Jesus' love, that same love stirs within us a deep desire to live in the glory of God—to abide in his will. That desire takes hold of us and we must cry out: "I have found hope! There is hope for all you somber and downtrodden! I have found hope!" At his last visit to Jerusalem, Jesus rides a donkey, and his followers and citizens of the city come out singing praises and exalting his advent. When he is charged to quiet the crowd, Jesus says, *"I tell you, if these were silent, the very stones would cry out"* (Luke 19:40). So is the moving of the rhythm of abiding. We mirror Jesus' sacrificial love for others. We engage in the pursuit of the lost sheep. We search for the lost coin. The love of God will not be contained but must overflow into the lives around us, for we are Christ's beloved and he is ours.

The Great Commission to *"Go and make disciples of all nations"*

(Matthew 28:18) isn't a complex formula of church discipline, theology, faith community, and persuasive rhetoric. It is sharing your life, in the rhythms of abiding and the rhythms of repentance with people. That's love, BTW.

CALLING A SPADE A SPADE

"For the wrath of God is revealed from heaven against all ungodliness and unrighteousness of men, who by their unrighteousness suppress the truth. For what can be known about God is plain to them, because God has shown it to them. For his invisible attributes, namely, his eternal power and divine nature, have been clearly perceived, ever since the creation of the world, in the things that have been made. So they are without excuse. For although they knew God, they did not honor him as God or give thanks to him, but they became futile in their thinking, and their foolish hearts were darkened. Claiming to be wise, they became fools, and exchanged the glory of the immortal God for images resembling mortal man and birds and animals and creeping things. Therefore God gave them up in the lusts of their hearts to impurity, to the dishonoring of their bodies among themselves, because they exchanged the truth about God for a lie and worshiped and served the creature rather than the Creator, who is blessed forever! Amen."

—Romans 1:18–25

Throughout our faith journey we are bombarded by sin, death, and the devil from every side. It seems they are masters of strategy and always find the weak link in our armor at the points of our vulnerability. The Law of God is given to break down the schemes of these spiritual enemies and prepare us for the Gospel. This is not a comfortable process because the wrath of God is revealed against sin and death in our lives. The discomfort of the situation moves us to try and resolve that discord. At this point, sin tries to dictate our next move—"You don't need to be uncomfortable. Everything you've done to this point is for your happiness. Sure, there have been some mistakes, but God wants you to be happy." It's always the trick to put sin's words in God's mouth. "God is love after all." Then you get to decide what "love" is. That is what Paul is describing in his letter to the Roman church. It is our sinful nature to suppress the truth by suggesting that sin isn't really sin and therefore not condemnable. In our attempt to err on the side of grace, we actually subvert it by creating no need for it.

We fear the legalism of past generations of Christianity and then fly to the other side by accepting sin as tolerable. We think we are enlightened, but this is not new (verse 22); it's futile. The first question of the Gospel is "Why does it matter to me that Jesus died for my sins?" If we don't call sin sin, if we accept it as it is, then there really isn't any need for forgiveness. Without forgiveness, those blessings of the Gospel—love, joy, peace, patience, kindness, goodness, faithfulness, gentleness, self-control[32]—are inaccessible. What we are left with is sexual immorality, impurity, sensuality, idolatry, sorcery, enmity, strife, jealousy, fits of anger, rivalries, dissensions, divisions, envy, drunkenness, orgies, and things like these.[33] These things are dead and spread throughout our lives into the lives of others. When our flesh is consumed with sin, in order to minimize the damage, we must be quick to call a spade a spade. *"For by works of the law no human being will be justified in his sight, since through the law comes knowledge of sin"* (Romans 3:20). We must let the Law do its work, namely, to judge sin and death in our lives, and as a result, recognize our need to be saved. It is in our brokenness that Jesus comes to us and preaches freedom.

"Come, everyone who thirsts, come to the waters; and he who has no money, come, buy and eat! Come, buy wine and milk without money and without price. Why do you spend your money for that which is not bread, and your labor for that which does not satisfy? Listen diligently to me, and eat what is good, and delight yourselves in rich food. Incline your ear, and come to me; hear, that your soul may live; and I will make with you an everlasting covenant, my steadfast, sure love for David."

—Isaiah 55:1–3

Jesus welcomes us without money and without price. He doesn't welcome us in our self-adorned wealth. We put on imitation designer brands, trying to pass them off as valuable. But Jesus welcomes us in our rags, to come and be satisfied. Let the Gospel be the Gospel.

How does the rubber hit the road? How do I call a spade a spade? It doesn't require us to judge people by the Law. It requires us to judge sin by the Law. You've heard the old saying, "Love the sinner, hate the sin." It's not that bad, but it's not sufficient either. Our job isn't just to hate sin, but to seek its resolution. The Pharisees hated sin but were satisfied in their self-righteousness (another spade). Jesus invites us to take our sins to Calvary, and leave them with him.[34] In light of the Gospel, we can look into the darkest circumstances in our lives and still find peace: *"[We] are justified by his grace as a gift, through the redemption that is in Christ Jesus, whom God put forward as a propitiation by his blood, to be received by faith"* (Romans 3:24–25). Keep your eyes on the grace of God in Christ Jesus, which will give you the freedom to call sin sin because you know where to find its forgiveness.

BRINGING THE LIGHT OF THE GOSPEL INTO THE DARK PLACES OF PEOPLE'S LIVES

"Therefore, having this ministry by the mercy of God, we do not lose heart. But we have renounced disgraceful, underhanded ways. We refuse to practice cunning or to tamper with God's word, but by the open statement of the truth we would commend ourselves to everyone's conscience in the sight of God. And even if our gospel is veiled, it is veiled to those who are perishing. In their case the god of this world has blinded the minds of the unbelievers, to keep them from seeing the light of the gospel of the glory of Christ, who is the image of God. For what we proclaim is not ourselves, but Jesus Christ as Lord, with ourselves as your servants for Jesus' sake. For God, who said, "Let light shine out of darkness," has shone in our hearts to give the light of the knowledge of the glory of God in the face of Jesus Christ."

—2 Corinthians 4:1–6

The Law and Gospel are important tools as we search for people in the darkness of their cells. It is with these tools that we call a spade a spade and lead people into repentance. We need not be persuasive in our presentation but honest and authentic. That means you need to spend enough time in relationship with the person to understand their situation. The rule is to always seek to understand before seeking to be understood. You cannot offer resolution for the sin that is waging war with them if you don't understand the battle.

Back in St. Louis, I sat across from Jack, who had gone through gender reassignment. He asked me if he would ever be welcome in my church when I became a pastor. Of course! That's the Gospel, but repentance was still waiting. He told me how he grew up never feeling like what was going on inside was in tune with his outside. So he got the surgery. He told me someday he wanted to be married and would like to have kids. I try to be honest when I have a stupid question, so I asked, "Can you have kids?" He said, "No, not biologically." I affirmed the idea of adopting because my wife was adopted, and I believe in the value of it. I didn't tell him he made the right decision or that God didn't care. The broken sinful world was already at work on him and had been throughout his life. So I told him, "In the resurrection, when your body is renewed, I can't tell you if you will have girl parts or guy parts. What I can tell you is that for the first time in your life, you will feel whole, and you will have peace, whatever that looks like." In that situation, I knew Jack desired biological children and a family but knew that wasn't attainable. Therefore, even with all the work he had done, he still didn't have peace.

Saint Augustine battled with sexuality his entire priestly career. He had many children out of wedlock with multiple women. In his writings he held tight to the forgiveness of sins in Jesus because he knew he was powerless to stop, so he waited on the LORD. Sometimes there will be victory in this season of life over sinful desires and attacks; sometimes there will not. Each of those moments has to be considered on a case-by-case basis. That is why this book will never be sufficient for discipleship because God promises to use people in relationship, not just words.

None of this process happens quickly. It happens over time and through developing relationships. Through that process we have to be willing to show our own struggles. People learn more from watching how we handle these situations than being taught the concept. So we have to be humble in our circumstances (the heart of repentance).

"But we have this treasure in jars of clay, to show that the surpassing power belongs to God and not to us. We are afflicted in every way, but not crushed; perplexed, but not driven to despair;

persecuted, but not forsaken; struck down, but not destroyed; always carrying in the body the death of Jesus, so that the life of Jesus may also be manifested in our bodies. For we who live are always being given over to death for Jesus' sake, so that the life of Jesus also may be manifested in our mortal flesh. So death is at work in us, but life in you."

—2 Corinthians 4:7–12

We are uniquely equipped to meet people. In the movie *The Guardian*, Kevin Costner is a veteran rescue swimmer in the Coast Guard assigned to train the young hotshot Ashton Kutcher (dude is from Iowa, represent!) to become a rescue swimmer. Costner is the best there ever was, and Kutcher has every intention of beating all of Costner's records. He asks him throughout the movie how many he saved: "What's your number?" "Twenty-two," he finally answers. Taken aback, Kutcher replies, "Twenty-two? That's not bad. It's not 200, but..." Costner interrupts him, "Twenty-two is the number of people I lost, Jake. The only number I kept track of." We have to learn that every soul, every person we meet, is an opportunity, and they all matter—even the hopeless cases. Kutcher asked him another question at the end of the movie: "When you can't save 'em all, how do you choose who lives?" Costner replies, "It's probably different for everybody, Jake. It's kind of simple for me though. I just take the first one I come to, or the weakest one in the group, and then I swim as fast and as hard as I can for as long as I can. And the sea takes the rest."

You have to learn to know when you can't get to someone, when it is going to jeopardize your ministry. If it is going to cost your marriage, your children, you have to decide when the risk is worth it and when you leave their soul to Jesus. I can't make that decision for you. I'm just your fellow rescue swimmer. But we know that we have more than we think to give. Jesus even promises, *"For whoever would save his life will lose it, but whoever loses his life for my sake will find it"* (Matthew 16:25) and *"Truly, I say to you, as you did it to one of the least of these my brothers, you did it to me"* (Matthew 25:40). Never forget, we serve others not because they are supremely worth it, but because Jesus is.

In this process we need to be trained, supported, and encouraged. Each of us needs someone(s) in our lives to disciple us and walk with us in this journey. At this point, you must consider how to plug into a faith community—how to find a group of Christians who will help you in this process and abide with you, eagerly waiting for our LORD's return in glory. The last chapter of this guide is directed at the process of finding, investigating, and then plugging into a healthy faith community. Not all faith communities are created equal, and many have serious DNA issues that offer cracks and crevices for sin, death, and the devil to fester and exploit. I will take you through this process and hopefully help you take the steps necessary to protect your heart and, consequently, your life.

TAKEAWAYS

JESUS' #1:   The number one reason Jesus died on the cross is to fulfill the will of his Father. It is Jesus' perfect completion of the Father's will that achieves our righteousness. So, when we place the value of the Gospel on ourselves, we sacrifice a worthy Savior.

CHRISTIAN LIFE: The good news "Gospel" is we have a relationship with the living God through Jesus. That relationship is about being, not doing. We strive to remember we are

Christian not by what we do but what Jesus did on our behalf. It's not about me; it's about him, and he has changed who we are and what God does through us (2 Corinthians 5:17–18).

The Holy Spirit teaches us God's will and ways and leads us to love one another.

PERSONAL MISSION: God has given us the Law and Gospel for our own growth but also to help others in their need, to speak truth into their lives, especially when sin, death, and the devil are trying to destroy them. You have been placed in your life by God to nurture your relationships and love your people.

ACTION POINT: Start praying, asking God to help you find a healthy faith community where you can plug in. In faith, step out and start looking for that place in your local area.

CHAPTER 16

Finding the Right Faith Community

BELIEFS, VALUES, ACTIONS

Extreme wrote a song in 1990 called, "More than Words." Classic. It may be on my karaoke list, not because it is a good karaoke song, but because I like slow, cheesy music (my travel playlist is like an elephant dart to the neck). Anyway, Extreme's *"More than Words"* is a song written to a romantic partner with the premise that the singer needs to see actions past words that show they are loved. The song is all about a person's actions, along the lines of "I Want to Know What Love Is," (but that's a different song). We are always trying to understand why people do what they do. Many people will look at a person's actions and assign their own motivations, usually with a condescending retort that questions the person's intelligence. This is a foolish practice because it only reveals your own ignorance. If you seek wisdom and insight, look for the motivations behind their actions to understand the deep-seated presumptions that create their world view. In our song, the singer is questioning the beliefs and values of their loved one. From the singer's perspective, their partner's actions do not line up with their expressed values and beliefs, so there is a problem in the relationship because the actions are communicating a different set of values that don't seem to be showing love to the singer. The good news in all this is that we got an awesome song. Actually, there are tons of ballads written about this exact challenge, where our actions don't line up with our expressed values or beliefs.

Here's the principle: beliefs determine your values, which dictate your actions. This formula allows us to trace through a person's actions (including our own) to understand what's going on in the heart and mind. If someone says they love you, you assume they value you as an object of their affection, which means they believe you are worthy of their love. Then they do something to hurt you, and you go into a tailspin because your assumptions about their values and beliefs don't line up with their actions. Through lots of heartache, you try to reevaluate their values and beliefs to adjust your own. The key to understanding people is to investigate their actions (the more, the better), what they say and do, to determine the various values they might hold. Many people say, "I love you" with varying values and beliefs behind the actions. Some will use those words to manipulate; they value what you can do for them, and they believe you can provide it.

This principle should also be applied to yourself. It is very useful when you are searching your own heart in the rhythm of repentance. Do my actions line up with what I say I believe and value in my spiritual life? If they don't line up, it's time to do some investigation because sin is probably hiding somewhere in your life. It's time for introspective soul searching, confession, and absolution. To be sure, sin doesn't only reside in our actions; in fact, most of the time it lives in our beliefs. If sin can distort your beliefs by providing false truth about who God is and how he works in your life, then sin can manipulate your values and actions away from the truth. Beliefs are also the hardest to change because they create the bedrock of our identity. So, with serious and fervent prayer, ask the Holy Spirit to work this process in you. For an extra point, ask someone you admire for their wisdom to help you search.[35]

> *"Search me, O God, and know my heart! Try me and know my thoughts! And see if there be any grievous way in me, and lead me in the way everlasting!"*

—Psalm 139:23-24

If beliefs, values, and actions work this way in a person, it will do the same in groups of people. It only gets trickier because groups will behave in unison, but values and beliefs will be all over the map. Therefore, when you begin to investigate a faith community, you must put in some intentional effort to understand the DNA of the organization, searching for the values and beliefs from multiple levels of the group. I learned this the hard way in my first call as pastor.

I have served two congregations since becoming a pastor, and during the interviews for both, I heard three things. First, the pastor is retiring after 30+ years at the church. Second, he is going to stay at the congregation. Third, we want a pastor who can bring in young families. In my first call, I should have been more concerned with the first two statements, but the last one always catches my attention. In today's church culture, many congregations are feeling the pressure of being an aging congregation and are looking for a silver bullet to come in and "fix" the problem. Most of my friends who serve in congregations around the country hear the same thing. However, it can be tricky to look past what they say they want in order to understand their true values and beliefs.

In my first congregation, the average age was over 65 when I got there, and they said they wanted to bring younger folks into the church. I took what they said they wanted at face value and was excited to find a congregation committed to reaching an unconnected generation. But during all four years of my ministry there, I constantly butted heads with the congregation because I didn't understand the values and beliefs behind the statement, "We want young people." What they valued was relief from the workload and the ability to maintain traditions. The other regular statement I heard was, "I already did my time. Let someone young do it." The truth is that many of the congregation had given years, even decades in service to the church. They were discouraged because there was no pipeline of volunteers to take over responsibilities. It was equally discouraging because they valued the traditions of the organization, and there would be no future generations to keep those traditions alive. They believed I could come in and find young people who valued and believed the same things the congregation did and would, therefore, do the things they wanted them to do. No change, just new people to relieve their discomfort. As you can imagine, all of us ended up disappointed and a little burned.

Whenever you are trying to teach or disciple someone, you must consider their circumstance and where best to apply the teaching. When dealing with small children or rudimentary principles, you focus on actions. When my kids were old enough to walk and too big to carry, I would tell them when leaving a store, "Don't go into the street." Later it switched to "Look both ways." I gave them directions because they needed to adjust their actions. I expected their response to be in line with my direction because they valued obedience to my directions—or at least they valued avoiding consequences. They believed Dad could deliver on those consequences, so they adjusted their behavior. I give them directions because I *value* their life and safety, and I *believe* that if they walk into oncoming traffic, they will lose. As they get older, I explain the importance of safety so they *value* it for themselves. Hopefully, if I've done my job, they will *believe* in the importance of safety, as it aids in maintaining life.

The same will happen as you seek to teach people disciplines and tenants of the faith. As you look to disciple, you often start by dealing with actions—do this or that and expect them to respond. However, you must also realize that if their values and even deeper beliefs don't match what you would suggest they do, then you will be spending more time at the beginning helping shape their beliefs and values. When I see someone's beliefs and values as described, not in sync with their actions, I do not point this out. Instead, I take them through a process of self-observation by asking intentional questions to help lead them to that realization for themselves. That helps them learn the process of confession and absolution. When you are better able to track and understand people's beliefs, values, and actions, it will also help you distinguish when the Law and the Gospel are being misused.

KILLING THE SPIRIT OF THE FAITHFUL: USING LAW WORDS TO TEACH THE GOSPEL

In this chapter, we will look at a common cultural flaw that is ingrained in many faith communities. If you haven't already read the chapters on Law and Gospel in this book, head there first. In today's Christian American culture, there have been some very disturbing traits spreading through many faith communities. Some of them are relatively new developments, and some have been around since the first century. Because the church is moving farther out of the mainstream and community relationships are deteriorating, it is crucial that we plug into the healthy faith communities that correctly use these wonderful gifts of God. When they are not used correctly, churches burn people. Sin, death, and the devil are given space to separate the sheep. The straight and narrow applies the Law of God and the Gospel of God correctly. However, if you fall to the left, you sacrifice the Law of God; and if you fall to the right, you sacrifice the Gospel of God. Being on one side or the other will kill the spirit and divide the people. The size and shape of the church won't tell you if their DNA is flawed. Neither will the history you have with the organization. You have to track beliefs, values, and actions with the purpose of the Law and Gospel. As you investigate faith communities to find one you can fit into, watch out for these hidden dragons.

Many churches confuse the Law and the Gospel by using Law words when talking about the Gospel. Regular Law words include "should," "ought," and "will." The Law words focus on you: your actions, your disposition, your decisions. If the pastor is talking about Jesus and being a Christian and then says, "You should do _____," he has turned the Gospel into a law. Darth Vader warned us that our feelings would betray us, but in this case, they could help.

If you hear the pastor (or anyone for that matter) talking about the Gospel and you hear words about Jesus, salvation, hope, etc., but also hear about your need for authentic emotional responses—but feel you don't measure up, or you don't have the hope he is describing—chances are he is falling into this trap. This is not a community you, or anyone who needs grace, should be a part of. This is a community of believers who are satisfied in their own abilities and performance; or at least they are faking it. If you spend any amount of time in this community, I assure you, salvation will always feel just out of grasp. One moment you will hear, "Salvation is a free gift," which is true. Next, you will be expected to prove it, which is not true.

Congregations that overemphasize commitment to the cause will fall to this flaw. Pastors who want to grow a big church can accidently overextend the congregation's resources and then use the Gospel to call to action. This can never be. The Gospel is complete in itself. The Law calls for action. There is no Gospel that requires your action. Remember both gifts were given out of love. Is the church, pastor, or leadership constantly asking for your money? Or all of your time? Are they pushy? Stop a moment and ask yourself, "What kind of Gospel is worth sacrificing for things?" This was the mistake of Esau and many leaders of the faith.

Some new friends of mine told me about a Bible study they had attended at the University of Nevada while they were students. It was sponsored by a local church but held on campus. Brian became a regular attender and later confessed that he had been kicked out of his home church because he was gay and that he currently didn't go to church. The leader of the group was astounded at the lack of mercy this man's church had extended to him. He promised that if Brian came to the sponsor's church, he would never be turned away. Brian started attending church for several months when one Sunday the pastor, without warning, called Brian up to stand before the congregation. After a brief introduction, the pastor asked Brian to publicly denounce his sexuality. Brian stood there silent, his shoulders slumped, his head down. I don't know how long he stood there, but eventually he walked down the aisle and out the doors with no confession.

Both churches confused Law and Gospel. Mercy is the work of the Gospel, but Brian's confession is a work of the Law. Regardless of if you believe homosexuality to be a sin, the point here is they handled it the wrong way. They applied the Law to sin, and what did it do? It killed Brian. How does God deal with sin? He applies the Gospel of Jesus Christ in his blood for our redemption. Brian should have been shown mercy and told that Jesus brings resolution to all his sins. Dealing with specific sin shouldn't be done in the public context, but rather in a small group or brotherly relationship. The problem remains in many congregations, as they kill the lowly and contrite, because they offer a self-righteous law rather than the mercy of the Gospel.

I've also heard it taught that we are justified by grace in Christ Jesus, which is a Gospel statement. But then they add ideas about levels of salvation and extra benefits to be earned in Heaven. In other words, the Law kills us in our sins and then the Gospel raises us to new life in Jesus. Then they go right back to the Law, as if it will do something different than kill us in our sins. Furthermore, "by the power of the Holy Spirit," we could somehow earn extra benefit before the Father in Heaven.[36] Tell me then, if this is the case, what could we possibly add to the work of Jesus? And if it is the Holy Spirit working within us, will we not be satisfied with his work and our reward? Does the Gospel bring hope or joy if you return to the Law to try and justify yourself all over again? Or does Jesus author and perfect the faith[37] that the Holy Spirit gives us,[38] which is the one faith that saves all of us?[39] I realize the grace of God is scandalous, in that it requires no manner of worth on behalf of the recipient; but that is the wealth of the Gospel and the joy of the world.

A TARNISHED TREASURE: IGNORING THE LAW TO EMPHASIZE THE GOSPEL

Some faith communities fall to the other side and, with the best intention, emphasize the Gospel. Keep in mind, the Gospel should be proclaimed with emphasis and more weight than the Law. It is the Gospel that defines the community and binds us in unity with God and each other. However, some have taken the path of least resistance in the proclamation of the Gospel by sacrificing the Law. Churches will proclaim, "No judgment here! We welcome everyone!" Maybe it's fear of declining membership numbers or being irrelevant. I think it's most often the desire to present the hope of Jesus to the world. But I regularly see faith communities trying to match the currents of secular culture. They get involved in politics (not social issues, to which the church should apply mercy) and try to prove they are a more enlightened group.

Don't confuse these changes with indifferent things like worship styles, times, and ministry focuses. I'm talking about when a church stops calling sin a sin and just says, "Jesus loves sinners." This is dangerous because the Gospel is true—Jesus loves sinners—but if we don't call sin a sin, then we forget that we are the sinners Jesus loves. The luster of the Gospel is tarnished because it becomes irrelevant; we can be loved because we deserve to be loved—we are worth it. If the church understands the Gospel and how to use it, then it should be able to present the Law in its entirety because it knows how to deal with dead sinners—Jesus.

The purpose of the Law is to kill us in our sins to make us aware of our need for Jesus. It illuminates the discord within us that points to the need for peace. If you find a church proclaiming the Law without the Gospel, you are in the wrong place. If a pastor kills you in your sin, that's okay and a good thing, as long as you are left at the feet of Jesus by the end. The Law makes us covetous of God's favor and love. It makes us search for the Gospel and covet it, like Gollum and the One Ring in *The Lord of the Rings*. He was content to be consumed by a river of lava because in his hands and to his heart he held his "precious."

The church that correctly handles the Law and Gospel will not have public communication concerning specific sins. It won't present the Law as the first interaction with a new person, because the church realizes that chances are, if a person is here, it's because they are looking for peace. They need to know this is where to find it. It will be open and honest in Bible study, preaching, and its many groups about what sin is. The church won't shy away from sin, but accept its relevance, and will bring people to the grace of God in Christ Jesus to give them peace and hope.

When You've Found a Pearl of Great Worth... Next Steps

WHAT TO LOOK FOR IN A FAITH COMMUNITY

You don't want to bounce from church to church or just attend services on a semi-regular basis. I did a year of internship in Florida, and we visited the beach a few times in St. Augustine. A day at the beach usually goes like this. You pack up the family and fight the traffic. Upon arrival, you get out of the car. It's hot and sunny with sand everywhere; people are trying to get all their stuff across a parking lot of cars, trying to find their spot on the beach. It's miserable, and you wonder how this could be worth it. But once you drag your cooler over the first sand dune, and you see the expanse of the ocean and feel the breeze, your spirit lifts as you begin to relax. A day of fun and time together awaits.

If the only time you spend with your faith community is one hour on Sunday mornings, it's like going to the beach and never leaving the parking lot. There are opportunities, and the best that community has to offer is waiting just over the hill. You need to knuckle down, grab your umbrella, and look for a place to set up camp. By now you should have some ideas about the beliefs that resonate with you. You can always do more research to figure out what your beliefs are to help you find a faith community to affirm those beliefs and challenge you spiritually.

GETTING CONNECTED—FINDING THE RIGHT RELATIONSHIPS

A faith community provides support for its members in three types of relationships. They support each other in their relationship with God, their relationship with each other, and their relationship with people outside their church. Most churches are strong at one of these and competent at another, but very rarely are they good at all three. Your job is not to find the perfect community; you will be sadly disappointed. Your job is to figure out if this community will help you develop relationships. Everyone needs relationships. We were not created to live in isolation (no matter how much sin and death wants us to believe it). We need a dynamic set of relationships ranging in size, purpose, and investment.

We need public relationships, which would be the congregation as a whole if it has more than 100 people at their regular events. These are people that we belong to without much investment. We don't know most of the group members' names or anything about them except they are part of the group. Sports offer these relationships for many Americans. You see someone wearing your team's shirt and you are excited and connected to that person because you are part of the same group. This type of relationship is exciting because you are part of something bigger than yourself, and that something is important. When checking out a church, ask yourself if you are excited to be part of this church. Do you believe in the mission and vision? Does the leadership inspire you? Every other group will still fit under the umbrella of the public group, so you have to check this one out first.

Next, we have large groups (30–80 people) that work together to accomplish something bigger than a small group can do. This level is like work relationships, where everyone is there serving a purpose and people know names and purposes within the large group. We need to be part of a group that accomplishes things too big for us to tackle alone or with a couple friends. It's where we make the most impact on issues. These kinds of groups are organized for the purpose of having an impact on a city at large. These kinds of groups run food banks, shelters, and English as a Second Language (ESL) programs. Since we all want to make a difference, look for the groups that are trying to make a difference and see if you would fit into that mission. Does your heart stir at the idea of meeting those goals? Is this something you could invest yourself in?

A faith community can be good at a lot of these groups, but it will never meet your needs if you can't find a small group to fit into. Small groups have 6 to 12 people, sometimes a couple more, who live life together. As they support each other through the rhythm of abiding in relationship, they are the closest relationships you have. You eat meals, you attend each other's events, you pray together, you cry together. These types of relationships are the building blocks of all society. We all crave them. Sitcoms are popular because they provide a placebo version of these relationships. Think about the most popular sitcoms through the years: *Friends, Cheers, The Big Bang Theory*. All of them have 6–12 people who are living life together. Do you connect with the characters?

Feel like they are kind of your friends? Are you excited to see them each week when they stop in? Are you depressed when the show goes on summer break or gets cancelled?

We all need those kinds of relationships, and your faith community has to provide them. Sometimes a church creates those groups very intentionally. We call them Oikos groups (family groups, not yogurt groups) in our faith community. Some churches let groups grow unintentionally, so you will have to look a little harder to tap into one of them. When you're trying to figure out if the church has a small group for you, look for one you can regularly attend with people you enjoy spending time with. Is there one in your neighborhood? Do they meet at a time that is convenient for your family? Ask if your household can all be part of the group. I find small groups are stronger when you can include your family.

Finally, look for close friends. I tell the guys I disciple that they need to find another brother who will walk through life with them. Someone they can share everything with. This is *not* your spouse because the truth is, you can't share everything with your spouse. Some burdens are not for them to carry. For example, one of my guys is struggling with an issue with another woman, a flirtation in its early stages. He needs a brother to walk with him through that sin issue. His wife will not be able to do that. The same goes for women. The best advice I can give is don't look for these kinds of relationships with the opposite sex. It opens space for temptation to creep in and cloud the platonic nature of the relationship, making it a romantic hybrid, which never works. Look for these people in your small group because the time spent in a small group will be time spent developing that close relationship as well.

FIRST INTERACTION WITH A FAITH COMMUNITY

It's time to crack out the iPad and do some Internet stalking. First, check the church's website. It would be wise to record your first impressions and thoughts about what this faith community might be like. Then dig into the website and look for activities and groups. Look for a congregation that has groups to meet all the needs we listed in the last section. Make notes about the groups that catch your eye and pique your interest for more information. That way, the first time you attend an event at the church, you can ask about those groups and maybe even meet a member.

You also want to find their beliefs page. Read about the statements of faith the church provides. If they don't have them on their website, make a note to get that information when you attend, or call the office to talk with a pastor. Check their Facebook page and see what people are saying. Don't trust the reviews on Google because they were more than likely scrubbed.

Once you decide to attend an event or worship service, plan to get there early and observe how the culture appears to be in line with the beliefs and values listed on the website. Check non-verbal cues, like building decor and where things are located. Spaces tell you a lot about the people who use them. Does it seem like they are kid friendly? Does it look like everything exciting they did was back in the 1960s? Do they have spaces to foster relationships? Most churches are pretty friendly, but not all churches are welcoming. You may have to extend your hand and introduce yourself because they want to give you space if you seem to be a new face. Remember to keep your posture open, smile at people, and make eye contact! Grab whatever materials they have available in the foyer to take home. Do they have a welcome card where you can leave your name, email, and contact information? Complete it and turn it in. How they respond to those cards will tell you about their values.

Once you've taken the time to investigate a faith community, you've put in the effort to understand the beliefs and values behind their actions, and you believe that this will be a group of Christians that will encourage you in your faith journey, it's time to take the next steps.

Look for groups where you can attend their events. Introduce yourself to people and begin making deeper connections. Meet with the pastor and have him explain the doctrinal beliefs of the church. As you grow deeper in your connection, make sure to look for and find the opportunity to grow in your relationship with God, others in the church, and folks outside the congregation. Build relationships on all these levels, and most importantly after all that, find someone you respect, someone who is further along in their faith journey. Ask that person to share with you how they got there. My prayer is that you will find the Living Water that flows through that community, which produces fruit in and out of season.

May the LORD bless you and keep you. May the LORD's face shine on you and be gracious unto you. May the LORD look upon you with favor and give you peace. Know that I have been praying for you and rejoice at the hope of being with you and our LORD Jesus.

"Blessed is the man who walks not in the counsel of the wicked, nor stands in the way of sinners, nor sits in the seat of scoffers; but his delight is in the law of the LORD, and on his law he meditates day and night. He is like a tree planted by streams of water that yields its fruit in its season, and its leaf does not wither. In all that he does, he prospers."

—Psalm 1:1–3

TAKEAWAYS

GOD'S LOVE: God's love is made known through his Church. It is the purpose of the Body of Christ to build one another up.

ACTION POINT: Do the research; get to know the church through their communication channels. Don't forget to get to know the people.

Remember, beliefs determine your values, which dictate your actions.

Ask them your questions. Here's one to get you started:
"What do you love about this church/group?"

RED FLAGS: Look past the surface level. A book's cover can be misleading.

Listen for the Law and the Gospel to make sure they get that right.

ACTION POINT: There are lots of things demanding your time and attention. You are going to have to say "no" to many things in order to say "yes" to your new faith community. Make these people a top priority because God has given them to you and you to them.

ENDNOTES

1. 2 Samuel 11:1
2. www.warinternational.com
3. John 11:4
4. www.mentalhealthamerica.net
5. John 10:8
6. James 1:15
7. 1 Timothy 3:6
8. *The Lion, the Witch, and the Wardrobe*, C.S. Lewis
9. *Luther's Works: Career of the Reformer*, volume 31, p. 56
10. Romans 1:20
11. Romans 2:13
12. Romans 7:10–11
13. Genesis 3:18
14. Romans 5:12–18
15. 1 Corinthians 13:8ff
16. Luke 22:42, Mark 14:36, Matthew 26:39
17. Hebrews 2:10, 5:7–9
18. Luke 5:8–25
19. In verses 9–11, all of these verbs are in the passive tense, meaning the subject is being worked upon not working.
20. John 13:1–5
21. John 13:32; 14:13; 15:7; 17:1, 4–5, 10
22. John 17:5, Revelation 5
23. John 14:1, 11–12, 29; 16:9, 27, 30–31; 17:8, 2–21
24. John 15:4–10, 16

25. John 13:34–35; 14:15, 21–24, 28; 15:9–13, 17–19; 16:27; 17:23–26
26. John 15:12; 13:34–35
27. 1 Peter 4:11
28. Hebrews 2:10
29. 1 Corinthians 15:24–28
30. Romans 8:31–39
31. Romans 12:1–2
32. Galatians 5:22
33. Galatians 5:19b–21a
34. 1 Peter 5:7
35. Matthew 18:20, Ecclesiastes 4:12
36. Ephesians 3:6–8
37. Hebrews 12:2
38. John 15:26; 1 Corinthians 12:3b; Matthew 16:17
39. Ephesians 4:1–7, note the singular "gift" of Christ in verse 7

For more information on the author, please visit
www.joshuabrownministries.com

Online resources include:
- Bible studies
- Vlogs
- Author speaking opportunities